D1257110

GREAT CANADIAN LIVES:

Portraits in Heroism
to 1867

Karen Ford   Janet MacLean   Barry Wansbrough

©Nelson Canada
A Division of International Thomson Limited, 1985
Published in Canada in 1985 by Nelson Canada,
A Division of International Thomson Limited
1120 Birchmount Road
Scarborough, Ontario M1K 5G4

Design: Bryan Mills & Associates Limited
Designer: Peter Wootton
Printing and Binding:
McLaren, Morris and Todd Limited
Typesetting: Trigraph Inc.

Canadian Cataloguing in Publication Data

Ford, Karen, 1956-
    Great Canadian lives: portraits in heroism to 1867

Includes index. ISBN 0-385-25011-8 (v.1)

1. Canada–Biography–Juvenile literature. 2. Heroes–
Canada–Biography–Juvenile literature. 3. Heroines–
Canada–Biography–Juvenile literature. I. MacLean,
Janet, 1954-   . II. Wansbrough, Michael B. (Michael
Barrett), 1935-   . III. Title.

FC25.F67 1985a   j971'.099'92   C85-099447-0
F1005.F67 1985a

Printed and bound in Canada
1 2 3 4 5 6 7 8 9 0/MTT/0 9 8 7 6 5

Acknowledgements

We would like to acknowledge the contributions in
writing and research of the following:
Mary McArthur Fraser
Barbara Hehner
Jeremy Hole
Jane Lind
Julia McArthur
Elma Schemenauer
Gloria Toth

Special thanks to:
David Anderson, Native Peoples Consultant
Baldwin Room Staff, Metropolitan Toronto
    Public Library
Jim Burant, Picture Division, Public Archives of
    Canada
Sharon Cook
Department of Ethnology, Royal Ontario Museum
John Grant
Ron Kirbyson
Keith Wilson

The cover illustration, by Greg Ruhl, shows David
Thompson and his family travelling through the Rocky
Mountains.

Permissions

209 "Thoughts from Underground" from *The Journals of Susanna Moodie* by Margaret Atwood, © Oxford University Press, 1970, reprinted by permission of Oxford University Press.

Picture Credits

The names of institutions have been abbreviated in
the following manner:

AGO Art Gallery of Ontario
CL Confederation Life Collection
CR Château Ramezay
GO Government of Ontario Art Collection
McC McCord Museum, McGill University, Montreal
MQ Musée du Québec
MTL Metropolitan Toronto Library
MTL(JRR) John Ross Robertson Collection
NGC National Gallery of Canada, Ottawa
NPG National Portrait Gallery

OA Ontario Archives
PABC Provincial Archives of British Columbia
PAC Public Archives of Canada
PAM Provincial Archives of Manitoba
PANS Provincial Archives of Nova Scotia
ROM Courtesy of the Royal Ontario Museum, Toronto

2 *The Journal of William E. Parry*; 3 **ROM**;
4 Raffi Anderian; 5 **MTL**; 6-7 Lorraine
Tuson; 8 **GO**; 9 Henry Van Der Linde; 10-
11 Steve Redman; 12 Laurie Wonfor; 13
GO; 14 **MTL (JRR)**; 15 **CL**; 16 Paul Morin;
17 **PAC** c17525; Helen Marioncu;

18 **PAC** c1144; **PAC** c11050; 19 **PAC** c12235; 20-21 Frances Clancy; 22-23 Greg Ruhl; 24 Chris Beaumont; 25 **MTL** T14867; Harvey Chan; 26 Bodleian Library, Oxford #50; 27 Reproduced by Courtesy of the Trustees of The British Museum K72731; 29715; 28-29 Mark Craig; 30 **PAC** c17727; 31 (detail) The Tate Gallery, London n1616; 32 Robert Johannsen; 34 Imperial Oil; 35 Archives of the Commonwealth, Boston; 36 **PAC** 23089; Henry Van Der Linde; 37 Henry Van Der Linde; 38 Colin Gillies; 39 Don Monkman; 40 Imperial Oil; 41 (detail) **PAC** c10622; 42 **MTL**; **PAC** c5750; 43 **PAC** c11016; 44 **PAC** c1410; 45 Steve Redman; 46 **CL**; 47 **GO**; 48 Heather Graham; 49 Chris Beaumont; 50 Résidence des Péres Jésuites; 51 **CL**; 52 **PAC** c11554; Robert Johannsen; 53 Robert Johannsen; 54 **PAC** c14360; 55 Emil Hustiu; 56-57 Dan Fell; 58 Musée Ursulines; **PAC**c10520; 59 (detail) Parks Canada Atlantic Region; 60-61 Laura Fernandez; 62-64 Steve Redman; 65 **PAC** c11237; 66 Anne Simpson; 68 **PAC** c10621; 69 **PAC** c20127; 70 Musée des Augustines de l'Hotel Dieu de Québec; **PAC** c10688; 71 **CL**; 72 **PAC** c34199; Robert Johannsen; 73 Robert Johannsen; 74-75 Scott McKowen; 76 Jody Hewgill; 77 Courtesy Frederic Remington Art Museum. All Rights Reserved; 78 Agnes Etherington Art Centre, Queen's University, Kingston. Gift of Mrs. John Irwin in memory of John Irwin; 79 June Lawrason; 80 **PAC** c7183; 81 **PAC** c13325; 82 **PAC**c1843; June Lawrason; 83 June Lawrason; 84 **PAC**c5660; 85 **PAC** c10687; 86 Musée de l'Eglise de Caughnawaga; 87 **CL**; 88 (detail) **NGC**6278; 89 **PAC** c69906; Denis Gagné; 91 Courtesy of Hudson's Bay Company C-69; 92 **PAC** c6896; Don Gauthier; 93 Don Gauthier; 94 Helen Marioncu; 95 **MQ** A50.1015; 96 Musée acadien de l'Université de Moncton; 97 **PANS** N629; Don Monkman; 98-99 Robert Lodder; 100 **PAC** c1226; Paul Morin; 101 **PAC** c1078; 102 (detail) **GO; PAC** c21457; 103 **PAC** c4263; 104 J. St. A. Warde, Squerryes Estate Office, Westerham, Kent; 105 **ROM**931. 26.1; 106 Garth Armstrong; 108 Chris Beaumont; 109 **PAC** c2834; Jody Hewgill; 110 Detroit Historical Museum; Ivan Kocsis; 111 Ivan Kocsis; 112 **PAC** c6150; Paul Zwolak; 113 Paul Zwolak; 114 John Knox, Seaplane Base, Lake Pleasant, New York; 115 Laura Fernandez; 116 Jody Hewgill; 117 **PAC** c251; 118 **PAC** c13182; Paul Zwolak; 119 Paul Zwolak; 120 **MTL** 1370; Paul Zwolak; 121 **OA**226; 122 **PAC** c33898; Marc Mireault; 123 Marc Mireault; 124 **PAC** c10350; Paul Zwolak; 125 Paul Zwolak; 126 (detail) Musée du Séminaire de Québec; (detail) **MQ**; 127 Bob Roach; 128 New Brunswick Museum; 129 **PAC** c70375; Leoung O'Young; 130 Universität Gottingen; 131 Steve Redman; 132-133 Mark Craig; 134-135 Laura Fernandez; 136-137 Colin Gillies; 138 Acadia Divinity College; Denis Gagné; 139 **PAC** c13415; 140 The Maritime Museum of British Columbia; 141 **PAC** c5536; 142 **PAC** c17726; David Bathurst; 143 David Bathurst; 144 **PABC** 7931; 145 Parks Canada, Department of the Environment; 146 **NPG**; 147 **CL**; 148 **GO**; 149 Jody Hewgill; 150 **PAC**c20053; Rick Jacobson; 151-153 Rick Jacobson; 154 **PAC**c2146; Paul Zwolak; 155-156 Paul Zwolak; 158 Courtesy of Philadelphia Maritime Museum; 159 Paul McCusker; 160 **GO**; 161 **PAC** c273; 162 Field Museum of Natural History; Paul McCusker; 163 **ROM**; 164 **PAC** c10717; Martha Robinson; 165 Martha Robinson; 166 **CR** 4320; 167 **CR** 38/359; 168 **ROM** 912.1.26; 169 **MTL(JRR)** 2750; Henry Van Der Linde; 170-171 Greg Ruhl; 172-173 Paul McCusker; 174-175 Henry Van Der Linde; 176 Saskatchewan Archives Board R. A. 537 (1); Marc Mireault; 177 (detail) **ROM** 912.1.24; 178 **PAM**; Paul McCusker; 179 Paul McCusker; 180 **PAC** c2653; 181 **PAC** c11069; 182 **OA** s.2328; Mark Craig; 183 Mark Craig; 184 **PAC** c11075; **PAC** c73725; 185 **PAC**c13392; 186 Archives Nationales du Québec N-474-36; Denis Gagné; 187 Denis Gagné; 188 **PAC** c1993; Paul McCusker; 189 Paul McCusker; 190 **CL**; 191 Newfoundland Museum; Mark Craig; 192 **PANS**; Paul Zwolak; 193 Paul Zwolak; 194 Molson Archives; Leoung O'Young; 195 United Church Archives, Victoria University, Toronto; Mark Summers; 196 **GO; McC**; 197 **GO**; 198-199 Mark Craig; 200 **PANS** 372; Paul McCusker; 201 Paul McCusker; 202 **AGO** PLAMONDON, Antoine: *La Chasse aux Tourtes*, 1853 2601; 203 **PAC** c6087; Courtesy of Special Collections, Dalhousie University Library; 204 Newfoundland Museum; **PAC**c28544; 205 Tania Craan; 206 **PAC** c6721; Mark Craig; 207 Mark Craig; 208 **PAC** c7043; Martha Robinson; 209 Martha Robinson; 210 **ROM** 912.1.101; 210 **AGO** KANE, Paul: *Indian Encampment on Lake Huron* c1845-50; 211 **NGC**6920; 212 **PAM**; Ross MacDonald; 214 **CL**; 215 Royal Army Medical College; 216 **PAC**c942; Pat Sayers; 217 Pat Sayers; 218 *Types of Canadian Women*, University of Toronto Library; Henry Van Der Linde; 219 Henry Van Der Linde; 220 **PAC**pa11852; 221 **PAC**pa103280; Martha Robinson; 222 Canada's Sports Hall of Fame; 223 Cincinnati Museum of Modern Art RAS CAM 48; 224 **PAC**c29977; Tim Stevens; 225 Tim Stevens; 226-227 **MTL**(Broadsides); 228-229 Frances Clancy; 230 **PABC**F641 19617; 231 National Museum of American Art, Smithsonian Institution: gift of Mrs. Joseph Harrison Jr; Paul McCusker; 232 Royal Geographical Society 3678; Paul McCusker; 233 Paul McCusker; 234 **PAM**; Shelagh Armstrong; 235 Shelagh Armstrong; 236 **PABC** A1233; Janet Wilson; 237 Janet Wilson; 238 **PABC** A1726; 239 **PABC** ppdp2612; 240 **PABC**A3081; **McC** M465; 241 **McC** M472 242 **PABC** A1124; Mark Craig; 243 **PABC** D7951; 244 **PAC** c36048; Janet Wilson; 245 Janet Wilson; 246-247 Alison Sloga; 248 National Map Collection 16701/232; 249 Don Gauthier; 250 **NPG**; 251 Glenbow Alberta Institute 6283; 252 **PAC** c6036; Martha Robinson; 253 Martha Robinson; 254 **MTL**; 255 Don Gauthier; 256 **NGC** 6673; 257 Tim Stevens; 258 **NGC** s111; 259 **AGO** KRIEGHOFF, Cornelius *The Blacksmith's Shop* 1871, T105; 260 **PAC** c6717; 261 **PAC** c14256; Denis Gagné; 262 **McC** M459; **PAC**c13969; 263 **PAC**; 264 **MTL** 2030; **PAC** c1732; 265 **PAC** c4572; 266 **CL**; 267 **OA** s1364; Paul McCusker; 268 **PAC** c10144; **PAC** c4814; **PAC** c4813; **PAC** PA334665; 269 **CL**; 270 **PAC** pa26370; Paul McCusker; 271 Paul McCusker; 272 **PAC** cl4246; Paul McCusker; 273 Paul McCusker; 274 **OA** s341; **PAC** c73723; 275 **PAC** c15369;**PAC** c83423

Dedication

This book is dedicated to Colonel and Mrs. Tom Lawson and the Lawson family of London, Ontario. It was Colonel Lawson's original idea to chronicle the lives of the builders of our nation in a format that would capture the imaginations of our youth. The qualities of those pioneers can show all of us ways to renew and strengthen the spirit of enterprise, tenacity, creativity and compassion upon which our nation is founded.

In supporting the development of this volume, Colonel Lawson has encouraged us to build upon the great wealth of our heritage.

Preface

This is a book about people.

You will find all kinds of people here—brave, wise, foolish or just plain lucky. You will find the famous and you will find men and women who just flitted briefly into the limelight.

What they have in common with us is a share in the Canadian experience. Like us, they knew the heat of our summers, the cold of Canadian winters, and the harsh beauty of this land. They are like us, too, because they believed in their own wisdom and they worried, like we do, about the future.

The people in this book are not entirely like us. Most of them knew Canada when it was younger. They saw a country in which dense forests covered much of the land. Huge trees pressed down to the very edge of lakes and streams. They lived in a world which moved at a foot pace. They travelled in frail canoes and sailing ships, at the mercy of wind and waves.

For the most part, they were tougher than we are. They took pain and early death for granted because there was no real medical science. Even the poorest present-day Canadian has better protection from cold, heat, hunger, and sickness than most of the people you will meet here.

Yet these are the people who made our modern lives possible. Their energy and experience, their wisdom and imagination created this Canada of ours.

This is not a book to read all at once. It is a book that might inspire you to a little organized day-dreaming, as you think about what it might be like to be Marguerite de Roberval, cast away by a cruel uncle, or Muquinna, facing strangers as alien and powerful as beings from outer space.

One thing about this book is sure. If anyone tells you that Canadians are a dull people with a boring history, you have in your hands the best possible answer.

Lucky you!

Desmond Morton

Table of Contents

Chapter One

A NEW FOUND LAND
Before 1600

The Mists of Time
Hoei Shin
Saint Brendan
An Igloolik Family
Leif Ericsson
Gudrid
Dekanawida
Robert Thorne the Elder

Across the High Seas
John Cabot
Gaspar Corte-Real
Giovanni da Verrazano
Jacques Cartier
Donnacona
Marguerite de Roberval

The Sea Dogs
Sir Humphrey Gilbert
Sir Martin Frobisher
John Davis
Henry Hudson
Peter Easton

THE MISTS OF TIME

The story of Canada begins long ago with the lives of its Native Peoples. Indians and Inuit hunted, fished, and farmed the land many thousands of years before Europeans came. They travelled freely over Canada's mountains, plains, lakes, rivers, and glaciers.

There were many different Native Peoples, each with its own language and customs. The Pacific Coast Indians fished for salmon and built great lodges of cedar. The Inuit of the North hunted caribou and built homes of snow. The Iroquois of the Eastern Woodlands travelled by canoe and planted corn, beans, and squash.

Despite their differences, Canada's Native Peoples had much in common. They lived in close harmony with nature and made full use of the materials nature supplied. They developed strict rules to survive through bitter winters and times of scarcity. They respected the lives of birds and animals, and seldom took more from nature than they needed.

Over the years, the Indians and Inuit produced their share of outstanding men and women. Countless individuals performed feats of skill and courage to improve the lives of their people. There were explorers and inventors, and great heroes and warriors. Today, almost all their life stories have been lost.

"An Inuk of Igloolik." The Inuit used the materials at hand to make all the necessities of life.

"Clal-lum Women Weaving A Blanket" by *Paul Kane*. Weaving was one of the many arts practised by the Indians of the North Pacific Coast. Like carving, it was often used to hand down stories and legends of the past.

Most Indians and Inuit valued their community very highly. They shared their food and put group interests above their own. They tried to hand down knowledge of their whole way of life, instead of the life stories of a few special people.

The Indians and Inuit did not write their history down in books. Instead, they followed an oral tradition. The elders of each tribe learned their history by heart and taught it to others before they died. After Europeans arrived, much of this knowledge was lost. Many elders died from disease and warfare, and many of their stories died with them.

Some ancient stories of heroes and heroines have survived to this day. They have been handed down in legends and songs, carved on totem poles, and painted on masks. These stories tell of people like "Nanabush" and "Copperwoman,"

who were half human and half god. Because these stories are so old, it is hard to know if they were based on real people. Only the legendary *Dekanawida* is believed to have really lived.

In other parts of the world, legends are told of the first non-Native explorers of Canada. Like the Native stories, these legends are shrouded in myth and uncertainty.

We know that *Hoei Shin* was a real person who sailed east from China in A.D. 458. We also know that *Saint Brendan* sailed west from Ireland 100 years later. However, we can only guess from stories of their travels that they reached the shores of Canada.

We know for certain that *Leif Ericsson* and *Gudrid* came to Canada with the Vikings around A.D. 1000. However, even their stories were not written down for over 200 years. We do not know where they landed or how long the Vikings stayed. The details of their lives appear only dimly, clouded over by the mists of time.

The Seafaring Monk

Hoei Shin was a Buddhist monk who lived more than 1500 years ago. He and four other monks left China in a small wooden boat. Perhaps they journeyed to distant lands to spread the word of Buddha, or perhaps they were blown off course by a typhoon gale.

Hoei Shin and the others drifted eastward across a vast open sea. After weeks of sailing, they reached the first of many strange new lands.

2 Next the monks came to a land they called Fu-Sang. They found trees with green flesh and thorns instead of leaves. The people wove "silk" from tree bark and used it to make their clothes. Fu-Sang may have been the coast of present-day British Columbia.

1 The monks landed first on an island of plenty, where the people marked their faces with tattoos. They sailed further east and found a land with rocky coasts. The people there were mild and peace-loving.

3 Hoei Shin spent 41 years wandering in the strange new lands. Then he returned to China, where his story was written down. Hoei Shin may have been the first non-Native to visit North America.

Brendan the Bold

A famous Irish legend tells of the travels of Saint Brendan, a devout Irish monk. According to the legend, "Brendan the Bold" sailed across stormy seas, tamed sea monsters, and found new lands. Many believe he may have reached the coast of North America.

Saint Brendan was a real man, who lived and died in the west of Ireland. He started a monastery in 558, with rules told to him by an angel in a vision. In 565, he set sail in a small animal-skin boat to find the "blessed isles of the saints." Then he and his men gave themselves up to the winds and currents of God.

Brendan had many strange and wonderful adventures on his travels. Some may have been imaginary, brought on by fasting and prayer. Others may have been real.

Brendan described a gigantic sea monster that "ploughed up the surface of water and shot out spray from its nostrils." Perhaps he was describing a whale. He also saw "floating pillars of crystal the colour of silver and hard as marble." These may have been icebergs, common in the waters off Newfoundland and Nova Scotia.

On shore, Brendan saw strange creatures with "cat-like heads, boar's tusks, and spotted bellies." These may well have been walruses.

Brendan found a new land and explored it for 40 days. He found it spacious, with many fruit trees. Then he sailed south to other lands, possibly Bermuda and Florida. He returned safely to Ireland with the story of his adventures. Over 300 years later, his story was written down.

There is no real proof that Brendan and his monks sailed to North America so long ago. We do know, however, that his journey could have been made. In 1976, an Englishman named Tim Severin built a boat just like Brendan's. He sailed it across the Atlantic and landed on the shores of Bermuda.

This map was drawn in the Middle Ages by monks. It shows Brendan saying Mass on the back of a giant sea monster.

AN IGLOOLIK FAMILY

It was a cold winter night in the wild northern lands of the Igloolik Inuit. In a cozy snow house, Howya sat teaching a game to her little brother, Pitseoluk. Mother and Grandmother sat nearby, mending sealskin boots by the flickering light of their oil lamps.

Howya's father and the other hunters had just finished two good days of hunting. Now the family were content. Their storeroom, a small snow tunnel leading off the main part of the igloo, was filled with seal and walrus.

Howya showed Pitseoluk how to play with the small animals carved of caribou bone. She dropped the animals on a piece of hide, and tried to make them land right-side-up facing her. As the children played, their father carved another little bird to add to the set.

When Mother finished her mending, she and Grandmother began to entertain the family with a game of "face pulling." Each woman tried to make a funnier face than the other. Mother and Grandmother wiggled their eyebrows, puffed out their cheeks, and bobbed their heads from side to side. They looked so silly that Howya laughed until she rolled on the floor.

Suddenly the dogs began to bark and a voice called out. Howya recognized the voice of Akavik. He and his family had come to spend the rest of the long winter evening. Howya's family welcomed their guests, and Father closed the igloo entrance again with a block of ice.

Father went to the storage tunnel and brought out a large chunk of frozen seal meat. He put it beside one of the lamps, along with a large flint knife. The guests knew they could help themselves and eat as much as they wanted.

As the guests settled down, the women and children began to play "cat's cradle." They passed around a sealskin string and made figures that looked like caribou, rabbits, and birds.

Through the long winter evening, the two families played games, made up songs, and told stories. The igloo became warmer because there were more people than usual inside it. When a part of the ceiling began to melt a bit, Mother put chunks of snow over the drips. Grandmother put out her warm seal-oil lamp.

Just as Howya was wishing Akavik would tell one of his stories, he moved away to the side of the igloo. He sat down in the storytelling manner, with his back turned to everyone in the room. Akavik then told Howya's favourite story, about how the raven got its black feathers.

As the hours passed, everyone began to grow sleepy. Outside, a strong wind was blowing. The dogs shuffled about and then crawled into the entrance tunnel to get out of the cold. The wind was too strong for anyone to go outside. As was the custom, Howya's father invited Akavik and his family to stay for the night.

Both families rolled up their outer clothes to use as pillows. Everyone climbed between layers of warm caribou hides, and Mother put out her lamp. As Howya drifted off to sleep, the only sound she heard was the howling of the wind. Another long winter evening had ended.

Bold Viking Explorer

Leif the Lucky was just a boy when he sailed on his first great adventure. In 986, he left Iceland with other Viking settlers to start a new colony in Greenland. Leif's father, Eric the Red, had discovered Greenland only a few years before.

As Leif grew older, he longed to discover new lands of his own. One day he heard the story of Bjarni, a trader from Iceland. Bjarni had been blown off course in a storm. He had sighted lands far to the west of Greenland.

Around the year 1000, Leif bought Bjarni's ship. With a crew of 35, he struck out bravely into unknown seas. After several days, he sighted land and went ashore. Leif found giant glaciers and a huge slab of rock. He named the place Helluland, or Land of Flat Rock.

Leif sailed further south and came to a land of forests and white, sandy beaches. He called this place Markland, which means Woodland. He may have reached the coast of present-day Labrador.

Leif and his Vikings kept sailing south. They soon reached another land, where the weather was warm and nature bountiful. Leif decided to spend the winter there, so he ordered his men to build houses. He may have reached the coast of Newfoundland, Nova Scotia, or New England.

Leif was delighted with the new land. The winter was mild, and the water teemed with salmon. Leif called the place Vinland, which may have meant "land of vines" or "land of pastures."

Leif sailed for home in the spring, his ship laden with timber and grapes. Soon after he reached Greenland, Eric the Red died. Leif took over as leader of the colony and gave up his life of adventure.

Leif's travels became famous and were described in songs and legends. Other Vikings visited the new lands. Over 200 years later, Leif's adventures were written down as part of the great Viking *Sagas*.

"Ericsson Discovers the New Land on the Coast of Nova Scotia" by G. A. Reid.

Woman of Adventure

Gudrid was just 20 when she left Iceland for the Vikings' wild new colony at Greenland. When she heard that *Leif Ericsson* had found other new lands, she longed to see them for herself.

A few years later, Gudrid married Karlsefni, a trader from Iceland. That same year, the couple led an expedition to found a colony in Vinland.

2 Gudrid spent three years at Straumsfjord. She helped organize the settlement and looked after it when her husband was away. She has been called the mother of Europe's first North American colony.

1 The Vikings reached Vinland and landed at a place they called Straumsfjord. A few months later, Gudrid gave birth to a baby boy, Snorri. This was the first European child to be born in North America.

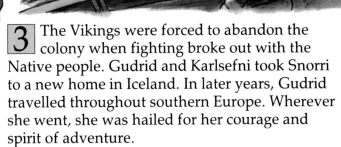

3 The Vikings were forced to abandon the colony when fighting broke out with the Native people. Gudrid and Karlsefni took Snorri to a new home in Iceland. In later years, Gudrid travelled throughout southern Europe. Wherever she went, she was hailed for her courage and spirit of adventure.

The Great Peacemaker

There are so many legends about Dekanawida that it is hard to know which are true. We are not even sure which century he lived in. We do know, however, that he is honoured as the founder of the great Iroquois League.

Dekanawida was born near present-day Kingston, Ontario. He belonged to the Huron tribe. When he was only a baby, his mother saw in a dream that he would cause the ruin of their people. She tried to drown him, but he survived. Hundreds of years later, the Iroquois League did force the Hurons to disband.

Dekanawida grew up dreaming of peace, not war. For hundreds of years, Indian tribes had fought wars and raided each other's camps. Dekanawida longed to end these wars and unite all the peoples of the world.

Dekanawida grew into a man and left the home of his family. He built a white stone canoe and crossed Lake Ontario to the south. He began to spread his dream of peace among the Iroquoian peoples.

Dekanawida's first convert was an evil murderer called Hiawatha. According to one legend, Dekanawida went to Hiawatha's lodge and found it empty. He climbed up on the roof and looked down through the smoke-hole. There he saw a large pot of water sitting on the fire.

Just then, Hiawatha came home. Looking in the pot, he saw the reflection of a face he thought was his own. The strength and beauty of the face made him feel ashamed.

Hiawatha decided the face was a vision, showing him how good he could become. He made up his mind never to kill another person. Then Dekanawida came into the lodge and explained his plans for peace. Hiawatha eagerly agreed to help.

Dekanawida took Hiawatha with him as his spokesman. They travelled from tribe to tribe, spreading their dream of peace among the Iroquois. A Seneca woman, Jakonsaseh, also helped them.

Dekanawida persuaded five tribes to stop fighting and form an alliance. This League of Five Nations included the Mohawks, the Onondaga, the Oneida, the Cayuga, and the Seneca. A sixth nation, the Tuscarora, joined much later, in the 1700s.

Dekanawida designed a way for all these tribes to live together in peace. League members had freedom of speech, freedom of belief, and the right to hunt on one another's lands. Each village took part in the decisions of its tribe. Every few months, chiefs from each tribe met to discuss their problems in peace.

Dekanawida's League of Five Nations was one of the first democracies. It may also have been the first to give women the right to vote. Hundreds of years later, the United States used the League as a model for its constitution.

After the League was founded, Dekanawida said goodbye to the Iroquois. He crossed Lake Onondaga in his white canoe and disappeared into the setting sun. Some legends say his work was finished and that his body lies buried on the Onondaga shore. Others say he left to spread his dream of peace to the ends of the earth.

ROBERT THORNE THE ELDER   d. 1519

Seeker of Hy-Brasil

In Irish mythology, the Isle of the Blest was also called Hy-Brasil. This legendary island was said to appear once every seven years. It arose somewhere in the mists far to the west of Ireland.

Robert Thorne was a bold merchant seaman from Bristol, England. He and other Bristol merchants badly wanted to find Hy-Brasil. Unlike *Saint Brendan*, they did not want to find the saints and ask them for blessings. They simply wanted to find new fishing grounds across the sea.

Thorne may have sailed with the Bristol ships that set out to find Hy-Brasil in 1480. That voyage ended in failure. Fierce storms drove the ships back to the coast of Ireland.

Thorne probably set out again around 1494. This time, he sailed with a partner, Hugh Eliot. Thorne and Eliot may well have reached the coast of Newfoundland. They may have fished on the Grand Banks off Newfoundland's shores.

No one knows for sure whether Thorne actually reached the New World. However, in 1497, the merchant John Day wrote a letter describing *John Cabot*'s voyage to Newfoundland. Day wrote:

> It is considered certain that this same point of land at another time was found and discovered by those of Bristol who found Hy-Brasil . . .

In 1527, Thorne's son Robert also wrote a letter. He claimed that his father,

> with another merchant of Bristol named Hughe Elliot, were the discoverers of the Newfound Landes.

Many historians believe Thorne's son was telling the truth. If so, then Robert Thorne the Elder discovered Canada at least three years before John Cabot. Thorne probably also went along on Cabot's first voyage of discovery to the New World.

In the 1400s, Europe seemed to explode with new ideas. The great European Renaissance, or "rebirth," had begun. New knowledge poured in from Africa and Asia. Old knowledge from ancient Greece and Rome was discovered.

All over Europe, artists, scientists, and philosophers began to make great leaps forward in their thinking. Suddenly people everywhere wanted to explore and understand their world.

This was a time of great prosperity. As Europeans grew richer, they began to crave more of the silks, spices, and gems of the Orient. For centuries, Arabs had carried these riches overland to ships on the Mediterranean. Then, in the mid-1400s, the Turks cut off these "silk roads" from the Far East.

European explorers began to search for a new route to the Orient. Some of them were firmly convinced that the world was round. They began to look westward for this new route to the East.

In 1492, Christopher Columbus crossed the Atlantic and reached the West Indies. Because he thought he had reached Asia, he called the people who lived there "Indians."

In 1497, *John Cabot* made the first formal European landing on the Atlantic coast of Canada. He was soon followed by a host of European fishermen. In 1534, *Jacques Cartier* was the first to pass beyond the coast. He sailed up the St. Lawrence River right into the heart of the new continent.

To the Indians and Inuit, the newcomers seemed both a blessing and a curse. The Europeans brought with them many useful tools and trade goods. They also began, slowly and steadily, to drive the Native Peoples from their lands.

The newcomers freely claimed land for Europe without consulting the Indians who already lived there.

Finder of a Newe Founde Launde

Giovanni Caboto, or "John Cabot," was a true citizen of the world. He was a master seaman who spent much of his life in the great seaport of Venice.

As a young man, Cabot crossed the Arabian desert to the Moslem city of Mecca. He saw camel trains laden with silks and spices from the Orient. He built globes to prove that the world was round and showed them to the kings and queens of Europe.

"Departure of the Cabots from Bristol." The name of Cabot's ship the *Matthew* was inspired by his wife Mattea.

In 1493, Cabot heard that Christopher Columbus had found land across the Atlantic. Cabot had long dreamed of sailing west around the world to reach Cathay (now China). He decided to search for Cathay across the North Atlantic, far north of Columbus' route. He convinced King Henry VII of England to support his plan.

In May 1497, Cabot set sail from Bristol, England, in a small ship called the *Matthew*. On June 24, after 50 days at sea, he sighted land. Cabot rowed ashore and claimed his "newe founde launde" for England. He probably landed on the eastern shore of Newfoundland or Nova Scotia. This was the first formal discovery of North America.

Cabot found signs that people already lived in the "new" land. Trees had been chopped down with an axe, and someone had mended nets with a needle. Someone had also set snares for animals.

Cabot did not find the silks and spices of Cathay, but he did find another sort of wealth. "The newe founde launde," he reported, "yeeldeth plenty of fish. . . . There is a great abundance of cod." Cabot's crew filled their baskets with fish just by lowering them into the water!

Cabot sailed further south, mapping the rocky coastline. Then he turned back to England, where he was welcomed as a hero. Cabot enjoyed his new fame, and he made the most of it. An observer wrote, "Great honour is paid him. He dresses in silk, and these English run after him like mad people."

"First British Flag in North America." When he was older, Sebastian Cabot boasted he had sailed with his father to discover the Newe Founde Launde. Historians now believe he was lying.

In 1498, Cabot made a new voyage across the sea. This time he led five ships to start a settlement in the new land. Over 200 men were on board, including some of Bristol's finest citizens. In Bristol harbour, crowds cheered as the ships set sail on this great adventure.

At this point, Cabot simply disappears from history. No one knows whether his ships ever returned. A few years later, one of *Gaspar Corte-Real's* men bought a pair of Venetian earrings from a Newfoundland Indian. These may well have belonged to Cabot.

For hundreds of years, Cabot's name was almost forgotten. His maps and writings were lost, and the credit for his voyages was given to his son, Sebastian. Today, however, John Cabot has been restored to his rightful place in history. He is remembered as the first European to make a formal landing on Canada's shores.

GASPAR CORTE-REAL   c. 1450–c. 1501

The Lost Explorer

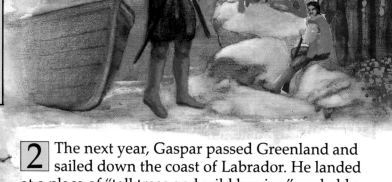

Gaspar Corte-Real came from a family of bold Portuguese seamen. His father, Joao, may even have reached the New World 20 years before Columbus.

In 1500, Gaspar set sail to find new lands for Portugal.

2 The next year, Gaspar passed Greenland and sailed down the coast of Labrador. He landed at a place of "tall trees and wild berries," probably Newfoundland. The place became known as "Codfish Land," because its waters teemed with cod.

3 Gaspar's ship never returned to Portugal. His brother, Miguel, searched for him, but he too was lost. In later years, many Portuguese fished the waters of Codfish Land. These were among the first settlers in the New World.

1 On his first voyage, Gaspar came within sight of the coast of Greenland. Ice floes stopped him from landing, but he made up his mind to try again.

GIOVANNI DA VERRAZANO   c. 1485–c. 1528

Mapping the Unknown

Giovanni da Verrazano was the son of a wealthy Italian family. As a young seaman, he visited many exotic places.

King François I of France was angry that Spain and Portugal had claimed so much of the New World. In 1524, he sent Verrazano to explore the lands across the North Atlantic.

2 Verrazano began to explore and map the North Atlantic coastline. He made several landings at present-day New England, Nova Scotia, and Cape Breton Island. He reached the coast of Newfoundland before he decided to return to France.

1 Verrazano battled fierce Atlantic storms in his small wooden ship, the *Dauphine*. After seven weeks at sea, he sighted "a new land never before seen." This was probably the coast of present-day North Carolina.

3 In all, Verrazano explored over 3000 kilometres of unknown coastline. He was the first European to report that the New World was not part of Asia.

Discoverer of the St. Lawrence

No authentic portrait of Cartier has survived. This one, by Henri Beau, was not painted until the late 1800s.

In 1534, Jacques Cartier set sail with two ships from the Breton seaport of St. Malo. The king of France had ordered him to find new lands full of gold and jewels.

Cartier crossed the Atlantic with fair winds and sailed through the Strait of Belle Isle. He found the rocky shores of Labrador harsh and forbidding.

I did not see one cartload of earth. I believe that this was the land God gave to Cain.

"Cartier Puts Up Cross at Gaspé." Cartier's quarrel with *Donnacona* set the stage for centuries of conflict between the Iroquois and the French.

Cartier became the first known European to enter the Gulf of St. Lawrence. He sailed around the gulf and erected a cross on Gaspé Peninsula.

An Iroquois chief, *Donnacona*, understood that Cartier was claiming the land for France. When Donnacona complained, Cartier seized him and his sons. He released Donnacona, but took two of his sons back with him to France.

A year later, Cartier sailed again to the New World. By now, Donnacona's sons had learned to speak French. They showed Cartier a great river (the St. Lawrence) leading westward to a freshwater sea.

The two Indians assured us that . . . one could make one's way so far up the river that they had never heard of anyone reaching the head of it.

Cartier followed the new river to the Iroquois village of Stadacona (now Quebec City). Donnacona greeted him warmly, thankful that his sons were safe.

Cartier sailed further upriver to the village of Hochelaga. There, he received a warm welcome.

There came to meet us, more than a thousand persons. . . . The men danced in one ring, the women in another, and the children also, apart by themselves.

Cartier climbed a great hill that rose behind the village. From its top, he could watch the river stretch as far as the eye could see. He named the hill Mount Royal, or Montreal.

Cartier returned downriver and wintered near Stadacona. That winter was bitterly cold.

All our beverages froze in their casks. And aboard our ships the decks were covered with four fingers' breadth of ice.

Almost all of Cartier's men caught scurvy from their lack of fresh food. By February, 25 had died. Then the Iroquois showed Cartier how to cure the disease with the bark and leaves of cedar trees.

Before Cartier left for France in the spring, he kidnapped Donnacona and some of his followers. He promised to bring them back the next year.

"The Virtue of the Tree Annedda." Cartier never described the tree that held the cure for scurvy. Many French settlers would die of the disease before the cure was found again.

Five years later, in 1541, Cartier returned to the New World. He visited Stadacona and Hochelaga, but he was not very welcome. Donnacona and the other Iroquois had died in France, probably of European diseases.

After a hard winter, Cartier and his men decided to return to France. They took with them a cargo full of gems and golden stones. Back in France, these turned out to be worthless quartz and pyrites. Cartier fell from favour with the king and never went to sea again.

The Kidnapped Chief

It was July 24, 1534. Chief Donnacona watched as *Jacques Cartier*'s men raised a high wooden cross on Gaspé Peninsula. Donnacona knew what the French newcomers were doing. They were laying claim to the land of his Iroquois people.

When the French went back to their ships, Donnacona and his sons followed in a canoe. Using sign language, he explained to Cartier that the land belonged to the Iroquois. Cartier's men forced the Indians to board their ship. Then Cartier convinced two of Donnacona's sons to sail with him to France.

A year later, Donnacona's sons guided Cartier up the St. Lawrence River. They reached Donnacona's village at Stadacona (now Quebec City). Donnacona was delighted to see that his sons were safe.

Donnacona hoped the French would stay at Stadacona to enrich his people. The French had many tools and weapons the Indians could use. He was not pleased when Cartier decided to travel upriver to Hochelaga (Montreal).

the kingdom of Saguenay. Cartier tricked the chief into visiting his fort, then ordered his men to seize him. The French also seized four other Indians, including Donnacona's two sons.

The people of Stadacona felt lost without their chief. They also felt angry and betrayed. They gathered their wealth together and offered it to Cartier as a ransom.

Cartier promised to return with Donnacona within 10 or 12 moons. Donnacona's people knew they were helpless to save him. They gathered together on the shore and bid their chief a sad farewell.

Donnacona went to France and visited the royal palace. He told the king of the wonderful kingdom of Saguenay, with all its riches.

A year passed, and then another. Still Donnacona could not return home. He and the other Indians grew sick with the diseases of Europe. At last Donnacona died in France, a captive among strangers.

When's Donnacona's people learned he was dead, they stopped trusting the French. Before long, the Iroquois and the French would become bitter enemies.

When the explorer returned, however, Donnacona quickly forgave him.

Donnacona entertained Cartier with wonderful tales of marvels in distant lands. He spoke of the fabulous kingdom of Saguenay, rich in gold and rubies. Cartier believed these stories and hoped to find this kingdom for France.

That winter was a hard one, especially for the French. Many of Cartier's men died of scurvy from their lack of fresh fruit and vegetables. Donnacona's men showed Cartier how to cure scurvy with the boiled bark and leaves of the white cedar.

In the spring, Cartier decided to kidnap Donnacona and take him to France. He wanted Donnacona to tell the French king his stories of

A Young Castaway

The young woman stood alone on the frozen rocky shore. One hand clutched a bearskin she had wrapped around her shoulders. The other hand shaded her eyes as she searched the sea. She had seen no ships for more than two years.

Now the young woman saw the sight she had prayed for. Quickly she lit the smoke fire she had kept ready on the shore. As the ships drew nearer, she shouted and waved.

The Breton fishermen on the ships wondered if the frantic, bedraggled woman was an evil spirit. This island had long been known as the Isle of Demons. Eventually they sent a small boat ashore. There they found a French noblewoman, Marguerite de Roberval. They took her on board and returned with her to France.

During the long sea voyage, Marguerite told the fishermen her strange story. We can imagine what she might have said.

"My uncle is Jean-François de la Roque, Sieur de Roberval. In 1541, the King of France asked him and *Jacques Cartier* to found a colony in Canada. My uncle invited me to go along on the voyage.

"I was overjoyed to be part of such a great adventure. I also had another reason for joy that my uncle did not guess. The man I loved was aboard my uncle's ship. My old servant Damienne kept watch so my uncle would never see us together. Yet somehow, near the shores of Newfoundland, he found out.

"My uncle became mad with rage. He said I must be punished for bringing shame to the family name. He put me and Damienne in a small boat and ordered us to go ashore on the Isle of Demons. My lover saw what was happening, and leapt into the boat with us. We were cut adrift, with only a few clothes, some tools, and some weapons.

"We built a log cabin and slept on cedar boughs. There was plenty of game. We knew that fishermen came regularly to these waters to catch cod, and we expected to be rescued soon. Winter began and still no ships came. My lover despaired. Finally he would not leave his bed, and he died. A month later my child was born.

"I could not give up, with the baby and my old servant to care for. I had learned how to use a gun and I became a good hunter. Once I shot three bears in one day, and one of them was as white as an egg. We spent a whole year like this. We always kept watch for a ship, but never saw one.

"Then came the black and dreadful time. First Damienne and then my child became sick with a fever and died. I prayed to God every day for the courage to continue. Then, mercifully, I saw your ships at last."

After she reached France, Marguerite told her story to Andrew Thevet, the French Royal Geographer. When *Samuel de Champlain* took over this post, he read Marguerite's story in Thevet's records. Champlain used this evidence to show that Europeans could indeed survive in the new land.

Under Queen Elizabeth I, England became the world's greatest sea power. Elizabeth achieved this with the help of a group of bold merchant seamen. These were her "sea dogs," daring swashbucklers who roamed the seas in search of high adventure.

Elizabeth loved her sea dogs and honoured them richly with knighthoods and favours. She looked the other way when they committed piracy and plundered the ships of Spain and France. After all, much of the booty from these ships found its way into the royal treasurehouse.

Elizabeth was delighted when some of her sea dogs began to search for the Northwest Passage. Like other European rulers, she longed to find a sea route to the riches of the Orient. Perhaps this route lay across the Arctic wilds of the New World.

Sir Humphrey Gilbert and *Sir Martin Frobisher* were among the first to believe in the Northwest Passage. Frobisher sailed as far as the southeast coast of Baffin Island. *John Davis* reached farther north, almost to present-day Lancaster Sound. *Henry Hudson* entered Hudson Bay before his men turned against him.

The sea dogs did not find the Northwest Passage to the Orient. However, they did learn a great deal about the northern lands of the New World. Europeans began to look more closely at the new land itself.

The New World was not the Orient, but it was rich in fish, furs, and precious metals. Many of its Native Peoples were friendly and eager for trade. Perhaps this New World was not just a

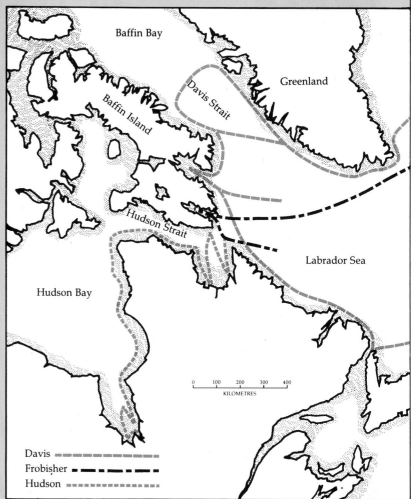

THE SEADOGS' SEARCH FOR THE NORTHWEST PASSAGE

barrier to the Orient. Perhaps it was worth claiming and exploring in its own right.

The Unlucky Explorer

Humphrey Gilbert was one of the first people to believe in a Northwest Passage through the New World. He was a brave and adventurous man, but not very practical. His first New World voyage was cut short because of leaky ships, poor supplies, and lawless crews. Queen Elizabeth called him "a man noted of not good hap by sea."

2 Gilbert sailed down the coast to search for a site for a colony. Then, near Sable Island, one of his ships ran aground. Most of the ship's men were killed, and morale fell very low. Gilbert decided to head for home.

1 Undaunted, Gilbert set sail again in 1583. He reached Newfoundland, but two of his five ships turned back. Gilbert claimed Newfoundland and other nearby lands for England. He made the settlers promise to obey English laws.

3 On his way to England, Gilbert ran into rough storms and heavy seas. He was last seen on deck, hailing his only other ship. "Courage!" he cried. "We are as near to heaven by sea as by land!" Soon after, he and his men vanished beneath the waves.

Pirate and Goldseeker

Martin Frobisher was a true "sea dog," a swashbuckling daredevil of the high seas. He first sailed when he was only 14, and he commanded his own ship by the age of 21. He was fired at by French cannons and held hostage by African tribesmen. He was also arrested three times for piracy.

Frobisher was soon known all over England for his great courage and daring. He began to look for new adventures that would bring him fame and fortune. He decided to search for the Northwest Passage across the Arctic wilds of the New World.

In June 1576, Frobisher set out with three small ships to find the Passage. From the start, the winds were against him. Near Greenland, a great storm blew up. One ship was lost, and the other turned back to London with the news that Frobisher had drowned.

Frobisher was still very much alive. He continued westward in his ship, the *Gabriell*, searching for a sign of land.

At the end of July, Frobisher sighted land at last. On August 11, he sailed into a deep inlet in present-day Baffin Island. He mistook this inlet for a channel leading through the Arctic. He called it Frobisher Strait—today it is known as Frobisher Bay.

Frobisher sailed about 250 kilometres into the bay. Then, in late August, some Inuit came to his ships to trade. The Inuit offered to lead him to a "great western sea." He hoped this would be the Pacific Ocean.

"Frobisher's Men in a Skirmish With Eskimos at Bloody Point" by John White. Some Native people viewed the Europeans as a welcome source of trade. Others, like these Inuit, saw them as powerful invaders.

Frobisher sent five men to follow the Inuit in a small boat. The men disappeared and never returned. The Inuit claimed to know nothing of their fate.

Frobisher waited and searched, but at last he was forced to give up. Summer was quickly fading, and he decided to leave for home. Before setting sail, he captured one of the Inuit. He also took a piece of black rock he had found on the shore.

Back in England, Frobisher was welcomed as a hero. The captive Inuk caused a great sensation. He put on a show for Queen Elizabeth and hunted royal swans on the palace pond. Sadly, the Inuk fell ill and died soon after.

Frobisher's black rock also caused a stir. When it was analysed, it was found to contain iron pyrites, or "fool's gold." However, one assayer claimed the rock contained real gold dust.

Word spread quickly, and soon merchants were anxious to invest in another voyage. Goldseekers vied eagerly for a place on Frobisher's ships. This was Canada's first gold rush.

In May 1577, Frobisher set sail with 3 ships and 120 goldseekers. They reached the islands of Frobisher Bay and began to dig for ore. In a few months, they returned to England with 200 tonnes of shiny black rock.

The next year, Frobisher set sail again. Once more, he and his men brought home 200 tonnes of ore. This time, however, mining experts showed that the ore was fool's gold—completely worthless.

Frobisher still had a dazzling career ahead of him. In the West Indies, he raided Spanish ships with Sir Francis Drake. He helped lead the British fleet against the Spanish Armada. He was knighted by Queen Elizabeth, and fatally wounded in battle. He died a hero, just as he had lived.

"Eskimo Man with Paddle" by John White. This is the earliest known Inuit portrait. It was painted by an artist aboard Frobisher's ship.

Pathfinder of the North

John Davis was still a boy when he first went to sea. He learned quickly, and soon grew into a fine seaman and navigator. Davis was a strong, good-natured man, with a natural flair for command.

Like many others, Davis believed in a Northwest Passage through the Arctic waters of the New World. In 1585, he set sail on his first voyage to find that Passage.

2 Davis sailed to Baffin Island and entered present-day Cumberland Sound. He thought this might be the Passage he was seeking, but heavy winds forced him back.

1 Davis landed on the coast of Greenland and met a group of Inuit. He ordered his musicians to play a tune and began "leaping and dancing" to the music. The Inuit were delighted and approached the English as friends.

3 On Davis's second voyage, he pushed farther north up the strait that bears his name. He kept careful notes on Inuit life and on the plants, animals, and climate. Once again he was forced back by ice and bad weather.

4 In 1587, Davis set sail on his last journey to the Arctic. Ice conditions in Davis Strait were very good that year. Davis sailed halfway up the Greenland coast—much farther north than any European had been.

6 Davis was a writer and inventor, as well as a great seaman. His book, *The Seaman's Secrets*, became a standard handbook for mariners. The quadrant he invented was used by navigators for well over 100 years. His record of his third voyage is still the model for ships' logs today.

5 On his way back south, Davis found the "furious overfall" of water that would be known as Hudson Strait. He correctly guessed that "the northern parts of America are all islands." He was sure that someday a Northwest Passage would be found.

7 Davis never returned to the Arctic, but he made many other exciting voyages. He explored South America, the South Pacific, and the coast of Southeast Asia. He was killed by Japanese pirates in the China Sea.

The Tragic Explorer

In 1610, Henry Hudson set out to search for a Northwest Passage through Arctic waters. He took with him a crew of 22, including his son John. Here is the story of the tragic journey, as the ship's butler, Abacuk Prickett, might have told it.

"Captain Hudson was a brave man, but a poor judge of men. We were only at sea a few weeks when the first quarrels broke out. The first mate, old Juet, picked a fight with Greene, the captain's favourite.

"In June, we sailed into the treacherous waters of an ice-clogged strait (Hudson Strait). Pack ice crashed around us and storms drove us without mercy. For over six weeks we crawled through those cruel, foaming waters. Our men grew sick with fear and clamoured to turn back.

"With great courage and seamanship, our captain guided us safely through. We emerged onto a great sea that we thought must be the Pacific. Then, after a month of good sailing, the open water came to an end. We were in a vast land-locked bay, and winter was almost upon us.

"That winter was one long nightmare. We ate anything to keep alive, even frogs and moss. We shivered in the cold, and many of us fell ill from scurvy. Juet and Greene began to speak against the captain, blaming him for all our hardships.

"Spring came at last, and the ice began to melt. We set sail in June, though some of us were too sick to stand. The captain divided up the last of the supplies and said they would have to last for weeks. There was only a bit of mouldy bread and rotten cheese for each of us.

"By this time, some of the men were already near mutiny. Greene stirred them up by spreading lies about the captain. He said the captain was hiding food away for himself and his son. He said the captain did not intend ever to sail for home.

"On the night of June 23, Greene came to my cabin and told me his plans for mutiny. I said I wanted no part of it, but I promised not to interfere. At daybreak, the mutiny began.

"Greene and the others showed no mercy. They forced Captain Hudson and his son into a small boat. Then they threw seven others into the boat after them. Some of these were loyal to the captain, and others were sick with scurvy.

"We cut the captain's boat to flounder on the bay. We left them without food, water or weapons. Then we hoisted sail and fled from the sight of our crime.

"Only misfortune awaited us. Greene and others were killed on Digges Island when they tried to steal food from the Inuit. Juet starved to death on the cruel journey back to England. Only a few of us survived to tell the story of poor Captain Hudson and his landlocked bay."

Whatever the fate of Hudson, his name has lived on. He is remembered as the discoverer of Hudson Bay, the world's largest inland sea.

"The Last Voyage of Hudson." This tragic scene shows Hudson's son John as a weak, helpless boy. In fact, John Hudson was an experienced young seaman of 19.

The Pirate of Harbour Grace

Under Queen Elizabeth I, many bold privateers plundered the ships of England's enemies. Then James I became king of England and made privateering illegal. Many privateers became pirates instead, raiding ships for their own fortune and glory.

Peter Easton was the greatest of these outlaw pirates. At the height of his career, he commanded 40 ships and controlled vast stretches of the open sea. He was a brilliant seaman, and sailors everywhere spoke his name with awe.

Easton built a fort and made his headquarters at Harbour Grace in Newfoundland. He raided the English fishing ships and robbed them of their supplies. He also forced many fishermen to become pirates on his ships.

Easton was never captured, though many countries tried. He decided to return to England, so he asked King James for a royal pardon. Easton was granted the pardon but it never reached him. After a while, he gave up hope of returning to his native land.

In 1613, Easton sailed into Villefranche (now Nice, France), the free port of the pirates. There he retired with over £2 000 000 in gold. He built himself a palace and married a wealthy, beautiful woman. He even got himself a title—the Marquis of Savoy.

Chapter Two

SETTLING THE LAND
1600 - 1663

By the year 1600, France was ready to send settlers to the New World. For a long time, the French had claimed ownership of Acadia (now Nova Scotia, New Brunswick, and part of Maine). Now the French king had to prove his title by starting a colony there.

In 1603, *Pierre de Monts* became governor of all French lands in the New World. He was ordered to start a strong French settlement somewhere in New France.

In 1604, de Monts set sail with his friend, *Jean de Poutrincourt*, and a young mapmaker, *Samuel de Champlain*. They first decided to build their colony on St. Croix Island (now in Maine). After a terrible winter, they moved the colony across the Bay of Fundy to present-day Nova Scotia. There they built Port Royal, on the fertile shores of the Annapolis Valley.

The first years at Port Royal were happy ones. Champlain started a group called the Order of Good Cheer. The members took turns preparing great banquets of fish and game.

In 1607, the French king decided Port Royal was not making enough profits in fish and furs. The settlers were ordered to abandon their colony. A few years later, Poutrincourt returned to Port Royal to try again. Then, in 1613, British raiders burned the colony to the ground.

For the next 150 years, France and Britain vied for control of Acadia. However, the French never entirely abandoned their colony. Gradually, an Acadian farming culture took root in the Annapolis Valley. Port Royal became Canada's first permanent European settlement.

The Order of Good Cheer was Canada's first social club. The Port Royal settlers took turns feasting one another through the long winter months.

PIERRE DE MONTS c. 1558–1628

Founder of Port Royal

In 1604, Pierre de Monts left France to start the first French colony in North America. For his site, he chose St. Croix Island, near the coast of present-day Maine. He thought the island would be mild and easy to defend. He had no idea of the dreadful winter ahead.

The first snows came in early October, driven by fierce gales. De Monts ordered his men to cut down all the island's trees for their fires. Soon only a row of cedars was left to act as a pitiful windbreak.

By December, ice floes churned all around the island. De Monts and his men were trapped, unable to cross to the mainland for fresh food or water. They dug into their last supplies and drank melted snow.

Everything froze, even indoors. De Monts' men had to chop up their cider with an axe. They chewed salt pork that was stiff as leather. As their wood ran out, they shivered inside, huddling together for warmth.

One man after another fell ill with scurvy. Their arms and legs swelled horribly, and their teeth began to drop out. Soon almost everyone had the disease. By the time winter was over, nearly half de Monts' men were dead.

In the spring, de Monts searched for a better site for his colony. At last he settled on Port Royal, on the shores of present-day Nova Scotia. This became the first permanent European colony north of Florida.

In 1607, de Monts was ordered to abandon Port Royal. He returned to France, but he helped others to explore and settle the New World. He urged colonists to return to Port Royal, and he helped *Samuel Champlain* start a new colony at Quebec.

Seigneur of Acadia

Jean de Poutrincourt spent his youth fighting for the glory of France. The French king called him one of the finest and bravest men in the land.

In 1604, Poutrincourt sailed for Acadia with his friend *Pierre de Monts*. Poutrincourt wanted to start a great farming settlement in the New World. He wanted to turn the Acadian wilds into another France.

2 Poutrincourt returned to France, leaving de Monts and his men at Saint Croix Island. After a terrible winter, de Monts moved his colony to Poutrincourt's land. He and his men built a fort and called their settlement Port Royal.

1 While exploring the Bay of Fundy, Poutrincourt and de Monts sighted a lovely, sheltered valley. Poutrincourt fell in love with the land and asked de Monts to grant it to him.

3 In 1606, Poutrincourt returned to Port Royal to take charge of the settlement. He ordered fields prepared and crops planted, and he developed the fur trade with the Micmac Indians. He also built North America's first water-driven flour mill.

4 Poutrincourt made friends with the nearby Micmac Indians and their old chief, *Membertou*. Several times, when food ran short, the Micmacs saved the colony from starvation.

6 In 1606, the French king ordered the settlers to abandon Port Royal. Poutrincourt loaded his ships with fish, corn, wheat—even live Canada geese! He took these back to France to prove the colony was worth keeping.

5 Poutrincourt arranged a rich social life for the little colony. He organized evenings of music, poetry, and story-telling. He hosted the Order of Good Cheer in his quarters and played music at its banquets.

7 Poutrincourt returned to Port Royal, but the colony was beset with problems. When he tried to raise funds for the colony in France, he was thrown into debtor's prison. Poutrincourt gave up his title to Port Royal, and died not long after.

Acadia's Black Settler

In 1606, *Jean de Poutrincourt* sailed for Port Royal with a hand-picked group of settlers. One of these was *Marc Lescarbot*, lawyer, poet, and scholar. Another was *Louis Hébert*, apothecary and farmer. A third was Matthieu Da Costa, already an expert in the language of the Micmac Indians.

No one knows how Da Costa spent his early life. He probably first sailed to North America as a slave on a Portuguese fishing ship. While trading with the Micmacs, he learned their language well enough to become a translator.

Perhaps Da Costa bought his way to freedom, or perhaps he managed to escape. Somehow he made his way to Paris in time to sail with Poutrincourt.

At Port Royal, Da Costa became *Champlain's* own interpreter. He went along on Champlain's journeys to explore the Atlantic coast. When he was at Port Royal, he helped to keep up the friendly relations between the French and the Micmacs.

Da Costa's work as translator did not last very long. After less than a year at Port Royal, he fell ill and died of scurvy. Today he is remembered as the first Black man to set foot on Canada's shores.

MEMBERTOU   d. 1611

Friend of Port Royal

The French settlers at Port Royal were lucky in many ways. They had mild winters, good soil, and plenty of fish and game. They also had the friendship of Chief Membertou and his Micmac Indians.

Membertou welcomed the French settlers and helped them to survive. He was a tall, bearded man, old but still strong. He became a good friend of *Poutrincourt*, *Lescarbot*, and *Champlain*. When the Order of Good Cheer met for its banquets, Membertou sat at the head table.

Membertou and his people taught the settlers where to hunt for game. They showed the French which plants to eat and which to use as medicine. One winter, Membertou saved the starving settlers by letting them live among his people.

Membertou could remember *Jacques Cartier*'s voyage to Acadia in 1534. This means he was well over 80 when Port Royal was built.

Despite his great age, Membertou was still a powerful warrior. In 1607, a Micmac was killed by another tribe while guiding Champlain. Membertou led a war-party across the Bay of Fundy and easily defeated his enemies.

In 1607, the king of France ordered the settlers to leave Port Royal. Membertou took care of the empty buildings for almost three years. When the French returned, they found the settlement just as they had left it.

In 1610, Membertou became the first Native Canadian to be baptized a Christian. He took the name "Henri," after the French king. His wife took the queen's name "Marie."

Membertou fell ill the next year, and died soon after. He was mourned by all of Port Royal, French and Micmac alike.

North America's First Playwright

Marc Lescarbot was furious. Despite his brilliance as a lawyer, he had just lost a case he should have won. As a grand gesture of outrage, he decided to leave Paris forever. He would join his client, *Jean de Poutrincourt*, and become a settler in the wilds of Acadia.

Lescarbot sailed to Port Royal and threw himself into his new life. He loved farming because it made him feel close to the soil. Often he dug and weeded long into the night, working by the light of the stars and moon.

Lescarbot also embraced the social life of the little colony. He made up poems to amuse the settlers and eagerly lent them books from his library. He also visited the nearby Micmacs and wrote down their songs and sayings.

In November 1606, Poutrincourt was returning to Port Royal after a long absence. As he approached the shore, he saw a bizarre vision. The Greek god Neptune rose up before him, waving his trident and shouting greetings.

This was Lescarbot's *Theater of Neptune*, with himself as writer, director, and star. As cannons roared and trumpets blared, Neptune sailed forward to greet his friend. Around him, French and Indian oarsmen were dressed up like fish. While Neptune sang verses of praise and greeting, they chanted a chorus of Micmac and French.

In 1607, the French colonists were forced to leave Port Royal. Lescarbot returned to Paris and took up his career as a lawyer.

Lescarbot was already North America's first playwright, first librarian, and first folklorist. Now he also became its first historian. In 1609, he published his colourful *History of New France*. The book was a great success, and Lescarbot became famous.

"First Play in North America." The Neptune Theatre in Halifax took its name from Lescarbot's *Théâtre de Neptune*.

In 1608, *Samuel de Champlain* sailed up the St. Lawrence River. He came to a place where the river narrowed, called the *kebek* by nearby Indians. Over 70 years earlier, *Jacques Cartier* had known this spot as Stadacona.

Champlain liked the *kebek* as soon as he saw it. A high overhanging cliff made it easy to defend in time of war. He ordered his men to chop down a grove of butternut trees. Then he set them to work building a fort, which he called the Habitation.

The first winter brought hardship and disease. Slowly, however, the colony of Quebec began to take root. The French began to trade for furs with nearby Indians. Brave young men, like *Etienne Brûlé* and *Jean Nicollet*, went to live among the Indians and learn their languages.

The French relied on the help and good will of the Hurons and Algonkins who lived near Quebec. To win their friendship, Champlain promised to help these people fight their enemies. He helped them raid Iroquois lands, and shot several chiefs and warriors. After this, the Iroquois and the French were at war.

In order to survive, Quebec had to become more than just a fur-trading post. Settlers were needed to raise families and farm the land. In 1617, *Louis and Marie Hébert* started Quebec's first farm. However, as the years passed, no new settlers followed.

In 1629, the French were forced to surrender Quebec to the British. Three years passed, then the colony was returned to France. Champlain returned in triumph, with French soldiers and French settlers.

At last France had agreed to support the struggling colony. For the next two years, Champlain watched happily as his settlement began to grow. By the time he died in 1635, the future of Quebec was assured.

"Madame Champlain Arrives at Quebec." *Champlain* hoped his wife *Hélène Boullé* would be happy in his rough young colony. She soon began to long for the elegant society of Paris.

Father of New France

A modern artist's idea of Champlain.

Samuel de Champlain was a true explorer, eager to venture into unknown lands. He was also a great leader who treated his men well. Champlain had one great dream, and he spent most of his life making it come true. He dreamed of creating a peaceful French colony on the wild shores of the St. Lawrence River.

Champlain fell in love with the St. Lawrence on his first journey there in 1603. Here are some highlights from the great career that followed.

July 1608. Champlain sailed up the St. Lawrence River to find a site for his fur-trading post. He reached a point where the river narrowed, called the *kebek* by nearby Indians. With its high overhanging cliff, the *kebek* was a natural fortress. Champlain ordered his men to chop down trees and build a "habitation" to live in. He soon began to call his new home "Quebec."

July 1609. To make friends with the nearby Algonkins and Hurons, Champlain agreed to fight their enemies, the Iroquois. He and his Indian allies headed south into Iroquois lands. Champlain fired his musket and killed several Iroquois warriors armed only with hatchets. From this point on, the French and Iroquois were at war.

August 1615. Champlain travelled with the Hurons up the Ottawa River and west to Georgian Bay. He became the first European to map and describe the Great Lakes. Near Lake Huron, Champlain met up with Father LeCaron, a French missionary. Together they celebrated the first Catholic mass in present-day Ontario.

"Champlain Overlooking Quebec."

This is Champlain's own sketch of his first battle against the Iroquois. The battle started a war with the Iroquois that lasted almost 100 years.

June 1618. Champlain watched with pleasure as *Louis and Marie Hébert* planted crops in the land they had cleared. At last Quebec was becoming a real colony, with settlers who farmed the land. Many more years would pass, however, before other farmers came to Quebec.

June 1620. Champlain brought his young wife, *Hélène Boullé*, to live with him at Quebec. Hélène was 22, and Champlain was over 50. Hélène would soon grow lonely in her new life. In only four years, she would leave New France forever.

July 1629. France and Britain were at war. For over a year, the British had been stopping supplies from reaching Quebec. After holding out as long as they could, Champlain and his starving colonists were forced to surrender the colony.

June 1633. After four long years in France, Champlain returned to his beloved Quebec. The British were gone, and Champlain began the long work of rebuilding. This time he would have more help. At last France had agreed to send more settlers and supplies. Champlain's dream was finally coming true.

December 1635. When Christmas Day dawned in the little colony, its great leader lay dead. Champlain had been ill for months, paralyzed by a stroke at age 68. The colonists mourned their leader deeply, and hundreds of Indians attended his funeral.

A Homesick Bride

Hélène Boullé was a child of 12 when she married *Samuel de Champlaïn*. She spent the first years of her marriage with her parents in Paris. Champlain returned to Quebec and waited for his bride to grow up.

Hélène hardly knew Champlain when she became his wife. She got to know him slowly and heard many stories of his adventures. He visited her when he came to Paris to raise support for his colony.

In 1620, Hélène left Paris to join her husband in New France. She was now 22 years old. Champlain felt she was ready to help him build his settlement.

After a hard journey, Hélène arrived at Quebec. She tried to like her new home, but she found the Habitation rough and draughty. As a gentlewoman in Paris, she had lived in ease and luxury. She found it hard to bear the hardships of life in a pioneer colony.

Hélène soon became very lonely. She turned for friendship to the Indians who lived near her home. She was kind and gracious to the Indian women, and she enjoyed teaching their children.

Hélène liked to wear a tiny mirror on a chain around her neck. The Indian children loved to see their faces reflected there. Once, a woman asked Hélène why she could see her face in the mirror. "Because you are always near my heart," was Hélène's gentle answer.

In 1624, Champlain took Hélène on a visit to Paris. When he returned to Quebec, he was alone.

Hélène stayed in Paris and never saw the Habitation again. After Champlain died, she entered a convent and became an Ursuline nun.

"Madame Champlain teaching Indian children." Hélène escaped her loneliness by teaching the Indian girls who lived near the colony.

Canada's First Pioneer Farmers

Louis Hébert was a druggist and doctor, but his first love was farming. He first went to New France as a settler at Port Royal. In 1616, *Champlain* invited him to become a doctor at Quebec. Louis gladly accepted, along with his wife, Marie, and their three children.

2 Marie started classes for Indian children and helped Louis care for the sick and injured. In 1627, Louis died after a fall on the ice. Marie decided to stay in Quebec and carry on their work.

3 In 1629, Champlain was forced to surrender Quebec to the British. Marie refused to leave her home and spent three years under British rule. At last, in 1632, Champlain returned to Quebec. He found his old friend safe and well, and as busy as ever.

1 Louis and Marie loved the pioneer life and the rich soil of Quebec. They cleared land, built a house, and began Canada's first pioneer farm. They grew ten acres of grain and vegetables to feed Champlain's hungry colonists.

First Coureur de Bois

Etienne Brûlé was a restless boy, who hated to follow rules. He dreamed of freedom and adventure far from his home in France. When he was just 16, he joined *Champlain*'s rough, young colony at Quebec. Soon, even life at Quebec seemed dull and tame.

In 1610, Champlain sent Brûlé to live with the Huron Indians. He told Brûlé to learn the Huron language and to explore the lands west of Quebec. Brûlé became Champlain's first "coureur de bois," or "runner of the woods."

Brûlé loved his new life among the Indians. He learned to live as a Huron, hunting for food and dressing in clothes of buckskin. He learned to move silently through the woods, and to shoot fierce rapids in a birchbark canoe.

In the next years, Brûlé ranged far and wide through the western wilderness. He went on many dangerous missions for Champlain and the French fur-traders. He was the first European to enter present-day Ontario and the first to see Lakes Ontario and Huron. He was probably also the first to see Lakes Superior and Erie.

Brûlé may have travelled as far northwest as Sault Ste. Marie. He may have gone as far southeast as Chesapeake Bay, on the coast of Virginia. No one knows for sure how far he journeyed. He kept no diary and made no maps of the new lands he saw. His only records were his

"Champlain in Huronia." Champlain sent Brûlé to explore the Huron Lands east of Georgian Bay. Brûlé was the first European to see Lake Huron.

own stories, which were incomplete and not always true.

On one of his journeys, Brûlé was captured by Iroquois warriors. The Iroquois were about to kill him when they suddenly changed their minds. According to Brûlé, the sky grew dark and thunder roared overhead. Brûlé cried out that the storm was a sign from heaven. After that, the Iroquois did not dare take his life.

More likely, however, Brûlé promised to make peace between the Iroquois and the French. He knew this promise would anger his Huron friends. He made up the story of the storm to explain why his life had been spared.

When he was 34, Brûlé settled down to a quiet life with the Hurons. Little was heard of him for three years. Then, in 1629, the British captured Quebec. With bitterness, Champlain learned that Frenchmen had guided the British ships up the St. Lawrence.

At the Saguenay River, Champlain met one of the traitors. He was dirty and unkempt, but his face was unmistakable. Etienne Brûlé had sold his countrymen to the British.

When Champlain accused him of treason, Brûlé hung his head with shame. He turned his back and walked slowly into the forest. No European ever saw him again.

In 1633, Champlain returned to Quebec. There he learned that Brûlé was dead. For some unknown reason, Brûlé's Huron friends had turned against him and killed him. Champlain still felt bitter at the treachery of his old friend. He told the Hurons he would not bother to avenge the murder of a traitor.

"Etienne Brûlé at the mouth of the Humber." Brûlé was also the first European to see Lake Ontario. He discovered the mouth of the Humber River and stood on the site of present-day Toronto.

Peacemaker and China Seeker

Jean Nicollet was a brave young man, with a gentle, peace-loving nature. When he was 19, he left France for the colony of Quebec. *Samuel de Champlain* sent Nicollet to live among the Algonkin Indians. He was ordered to learn Indian languages and to explore new lands for France.

1 Nicollet spent the next 16 years among the Algonkin, Huron, and Nipissing tribes. He explored the Indians' lands and won their friendship for France. He learned a great deal about Indian customs and kept careful notes in a journal.

2 In 1634, Nicollet set out to make peace with the Winnebago Indians, near present-day Lake Michigan. Because he hoped to find a way to China, he took along a robe of Chinese silk. Nicollet searched almost to the Mississippi River, further west than any European had been.

3 Nicollet spent his last years in the new French colony at Trois Rivières. He worked in the fur trade and acted as interpreter for the missionaries. He drowned on a mission of peace, while hurrying to save an Iroquois prisoner from the Hurons.

FAITH AND FURS

In 1609, *Samuel de Champlain* sided with the Hurons against their enemies, the Iroquois. He took part in a raid of Iroquois lands and shot two Iroquois chiefs. From that point on, the French and Hurons were partners in the fur trade. The French and the Iroquois were bitter enemies.

As the years passed, the French moved west into the Huron lands around Georgian Bay. Some went to trade for furs, others to preach Christianity. As the French moved west, they brought with them many diseases. Thousands of Hurons died, until only a third of them were left.

In the 1630s, black-robed Jesuit priests built their first missions in Huronia. They preached the Catholic faith and took care of the sick and dying Hurons. They wrote about their adventures in a journal called the *Jesuit Relations*.

The *Relations* inspired many French people to settle in New France. In 1642, a group of devout men and women decided to start a mission settlement. Led by *Paul de Maisonneuve*, they sailed up the St. Lawrence River. They built a fort and named their little colony Ville-Marie. Later, it would be known as Montreal.

In 1649, the Iroquois launched a full-scale invasion of Huronia. They attacked the Jesuit missions and captured the priests, including *Jean de Brébeuf*. Many Hurons died in battle, and the rest were forced to flee. Ravaged by disease and scattered by warfare, the Hurons lost their power as a people.

Over the next years, the French and Iroquois continued their war. Each group wanted control of the lands north of the Great Lakes. On both sides, there was bravery and cruelty. There were also many who worked for peace, including *Jeanne Mance* and *Garakontié*.

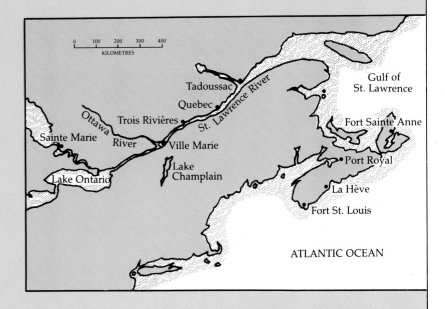

FRENCH SETTLEMENTS IN NORTHEASTERN NORTH AMERICA, 1650

Martyr at Huronia

Jean de Brébeuf was a giant of a man, with broad shoulders and a black bushy beard. He was a "Blackrobe," a Jesuit priest who came from France to convert the Indians. He was a strong, brave man, with a kind heart and a deep sense of purpose.

Brébeuf came to New France in 1625, eager to begin work. He journeyed far into Huronia, the Huron lands around Georgian Bay. He learned to live as the Hurons did, camping in the forests and hunting for his food. He had a gift for languages and could soon understand Huron very well.

When the British captured Quebec in 1629, Brébeuf was forced to leave New France. He returned in 1633, as soon as the British were gone. This time, he wanted to build missions deep in Huronia.

In the next years, Brébeuf worked tirelessly among the Hurons. He studied their language and beliefs, and he put together a Huron dictionary. He built missions and organized priests to spread the teachings of the Catholic faith. He translated prayers into Huron, and wrote the world's first Huron Christmas carol.

Brébeuf grew to love and admire the Huron people. Here is a passage from one of his reports back to France.

> You note, in the first place, a great love and union among them. Their hospitality toward all sorts of strangers is remarkable. . . . They never close the door upon a stranger, and once having received him into their homes, they share with him the best they have.

These were cruel years for the Hurons. Smallpox and influenza spread through their villages, killing two-thirds of their people. Many

"Sainte Marie Among the Hurons." The Jesuits built this mission as their headquarters in Huronia. In 1649, they burnt it down rather than surrender it to the Iroquois.

Hurons blamed the priests for bringing the European diseases. Brébeuf tended the sick and dying and slowly won the Hurons' trust.

In the 1640s, the Iroquois launched a full-scale war against the Hurons. Like the French, the Iroquois wanted to control the lands north of the Great Lakes.

In 1649, the Iroquois struck deep in the heart of Huronia. A thousand warriors attacked the mission where Brébeuf was staying. As the battle raged around him, Brébeuf went on calmly with his work. He nursed the wounded Hurons and offered prayers for those who were dying.

The Iroquois captured Brébeuf, then tortured and killed him. Brébeuf met his death bravely, without crying out. Even his Iroquois captors admired his strength and courage. When news of his bravery spread, many Indians were drawn to the Catholic faith.

Almost 300 years after Brébeuf's death, his memory was honoured by the Catholic Church. Along with other Jesuits, Father Brébeuf became a patron saint of Canada.

Founder of Montreal

Paul de Maisonneuve was a brave, quiet man, with a deep faith in his religion. He became a soldier at 13, and was already retired at 30. That same year, he agreed to start a Catholic settlement at Montreal.

De Maisonneuve wanted to bring his faith deep into Indian lands. He did not care that his colony would be right on the Iroquois trading route.

2 In 1642, de Maisonneuve and his settlers landed at Montreal. They celebrated mass, then set to work building their new home. De Maisonneuve cut down the first tree himself. His settlers called their colony "Ville-Marie."

3 On Christmas Eve, the St. Lawrence River flooded parts of Ville-Marie. As the waters rose, de Maisonneuve swore to plant a cross on Mount Royal if the colony was saved. The waters subsided, and two weeks later de Maisonneuve carried his cross up the mountain.

1 De Maisonneuve arrived at Quebec in 1641. The colonists there opposed his plans and called him foolhardy. De Maisonneuve replied that he would go to Montreal "even if all its trees were to change into Iroquois."

4 The Iroquois soon began to attack Ville-Marie. After several raids, de Maisonneuve decided to fight back. He led 30 men into the woods, but they were badly outnumbered. De Maisonneuve bravely stood his ground and guarded his men as they ran back to the fort.

5 De Maisonneuve governed wisely and kept order in the growing colony. He ordered brawlers to pay the medical bills of their victims. He also ordered slanderers to praise each other in public.

6 As the years passed, Iroquois raids became more frequent. De Maisonneuve went to France and returned with over 100 soldiers. After this, the Iroquois found it harder to attack the colony. Slowly, they began to make peace.

7 In 1665, de Maisonneuve was suddenly ordered to return to France. He left sadly, as the settlers wept and waved goodbye. In France, he retired to his country estate. There he built a rough cabin to remind him of life in Ville-Marie.

The Angel of Ville-Marie

Jeanne Mance arrived at Ville-Marie with *Paul de Maisonneuve* in 1642. With money she had raised in France, she built a hospital outside the fort. This four-room hospital, the "Hotel Dieu," was soon filled with the victims of war and disease.

Here is how a sick Algonkin girl might have described Jeanne Mance and her hospital.

"The noise is terrible, like a great storm raging outside the walls. The thunder and lightning are the flash and roar of guns. I can hear the war cries of the Iroquois and horrible screams from both sides.

"My name is Little Faun and I am 11 years old. Two weeks ago I was near death with the spotted fever (smallpox). My mother carried me here on her back, for she had heard of Sister Jeanne's healing skills.

"I remember Sister Jeanne sitting by me through the long nights, stroking my forehead with her cool hand. I remember her calm voice soothing me in Algonkin, telling me I would soon be well.

"After the fever lifted, I began to look around me. I was amazed to see a wounded Iroquois in this place. Sister Jeanne gives him the same care that she gives her people and mine. When I asked her why, she said we must all learn to love our enemies.

"Today I told Sister Jeanne I would stay and help her when I'm better. She hardly has time to eat or sleep, she works so hard. Sister Jeanne just laughed and shook her head. She said that soon I must go home to the peace and safety of my village."

Jeanne Mance lived to see the colony at Ville-Marie grow strong and secure. In all, she spent more than 30 years tending the sick and wounded of New France.

Gallant Huron Chief

As a young man, Annaotaha saw two-thirds of his people die. Almost 20 000 Hurons were killed by diseases brought from Europe by the French. Then, to make things worse, the Iroquois invaded Huron lands.

Annaotaha could not fight smallpox, but he could fight the Iroquois. He risked his life many times in bold and daring raids. He won many battles, but the Hurons lost their war. By 1649, they were all but finished as a people.

Annaotaha was at the mission of *Jean de Brébeuf* when 1000 Iroquois warriors attacked. He fought gallantly to defend the mission, but his men were hopelessly outnumbered.

When their lands were lost, Annaotaha and other Hurons took refuge on an island in Georgian Bay. That winter, many refugees were killed by famine, disease, and Iroquois ambush. Annaotaha was taken prisoner, but he managed to trick and kill his Iroquois captors.

In 1660, Annaotaha set out from Quebec with 40 Huron warriors. They were on their way to ambush Iroquois canoes on the Ottawa River. They joined forces with a small group of Frenchmen led by Adam Dollard. Soon after, the Hurons and French met a war party of 200 Iroquois.

Annaotaha and Dollard fought well. They held out against the Iroquois for seven long days. Then 500 more Iroquois arrived, and Annaotaha knew he had lost.

Annaotaha sent out a truce party to discuss terms for surrender. When an Iroquois truce party returned, the French panicked and fired their guns. "Ah comrades," sighed Annaotaha. "You have spoilt everything. You ought to have awaited the result of the council."

The Iroquois were outraged at the attack on their truce party. They launched a last fierce attack on the French and Hurons. Annaotaha died fighting, the last great chief of his people.

An Iroquois Peacemaker

For almost 100 years, the French and the Iroquois fought for the lands north of the Great Lakes. On both sides, there were terrible acts of cruelty and violence. On both sides, there were also men and women who worked for peace.

Garakontié belonged to the Onondaga tribe, one of the nations of the Iroquois League. He was not born a chief, but he became well-known for his honesty and wisdom. He was a calm, patient man, with a deep pride in his Iroquois traditions.

Garakontié believed that war with the French was doing his people great harm. He could see that the French colonies were growing and getting stronger. Many Iroquois, meanwhile, were dying from warfare and the diseases from Europe.

In 1658, a Jesuit priest named Simon Le Moyne journeyed into Iroquois lands. Le Moyne wanted to release the French prisoners held in Iroquois villages. He also wanted to find a way to end the long war.

Like Garakontié, Le Moyne was a man of peace. The two men soon became close friends. Garakontié persuaded the Iroquois to release two French prisoners. In return, the French released two Iroquois held captive in Montreal.

Garakontié refused to become a Christian, but he worked closely with Le Moyne. He brought the priest into his lodge, built a chapel for him, and protected him from harm. He encouraged other Iroquois to listen to Le Moyne's words of peace.

In 1661, Garakontié helped organize a truce between the western Iroquois and the French. That same year, he took nine French prisoners to Montreal to exchange them for captive Iroquois.

On his way to Montreal, Garakontié learned that fighting had broken out near the town. His followers grew frightened and pleaded with him to turn back. Garakontié refused, and bravely went forward to meet the enemy on his mission of peace.

Garakontié wanted peace, but he was not willing to sacrifice the interests of his people. He wanted to make sure that Iroquois lands and Iroquois rights were respected. He was a clever politician, and he drove a hard bargain. Over the years, he helped arrange many periods of truce in the long war.

In 1673, Garakontié and other Iroquois leaders met with *Governor Frontenac* on the shores of Lake Ontario. Garakontié was the first to speak. His words dazzled Frontenac, and forced him into a maze of complex negotiations. Later, Frontenac claimed to be astonished by "the eloquence, the shrewdness, and the finesse" of the Iroquois diplomats.

When Garakontié died, it seemed that peace had come to the Iroquois at last. However, this was not to be. Another 23 years of warfare would pass before Garakontié's dream of peace would finally come true.

Teacher in New France

When Marie de La Peltrie was a young girl, she had a vision that told her to go to New France. Her wealthy father did not like the idea. He forced her to get married against her will when she was 17.

When Marie's husband died, her father ordered her to marry again. He said he would cut her out of his will if she disobeyed. Marie wanted to use the money to help others. She tricked her father by arranging a false marriage with an old friend.

When Marie's father died, she was free at last to live as she wanted. In 1639, she set sail for Quebec. For the next three years, she worked hard to set up an Ursuline convent and school. She loved teaching the young Indian girls, and she greeted them with kisses.

In May 1642, Marie went with *Paul de Maisonneuve* to start a Catholic settlement at Montreal. Marie lived for four years at Ville-Marie. Although her health was poor, she always did her share of the hard and menial work.

Marie's little dog, Pilote, also played an important part at Ville-Marie. Pilote barked loudly to warn the settlers whenever strangers were in the area!

Marie returned to Quebec in 1646. She built herself a tiny house next to her beloved school. There she lived for the rest of her life.

Marie was a very rich woman, but she gave almost all her money away. She wore a grey uniform that was always patched and threadbare. Once someone told her she should give these worn-out garments to the poor. "I prefer to see the poor in *new* clothes," replied Marie.

"First Ursuline nuns with Indian pupils at Quebec." Marie de la Peltrie never became a nun but she is considered a foundress of the Ursuline convent.

EARLY ACADIA

In 1613, British raiders destroyed the French colony at Port Royal. The British now laid claim to Acadia (New Brunswick, Nova Scotia, and part of Maine). However, the French refused to abandon their Acadian lands. Some, like *Charles de La Tour*, took to the woods and kept control of the fur trade.

In 1621, the British made William Alexander, a Scottish poet, the governor of Acadia. Alexander changed the land's name to New Scotland, or Nova Scotia. He started a settlement, but it lasted only a few years.

In 1632, Acadia was returned to France. Charles de La Tour had led the French settlers through much of the long struggle with Britain. His leadership was soon challenged, however, by Charles D'Aulnay, a governor from France.

For over ten years, the two men feuded bitterly to control the colony. In 1645, D'Aulnay defeated La Tour's wife, *Marie*, in a final battle. D'Aulnay drowned five years later, however, and La Tour became Acadia's governor.

In 1654, the English took Acadia yet again. For the next 100 years, France and England would vie for control of the colony. Acadia would become the most contested land in all of North America.

Despite these conflicts, farms slowly spread along Acadia's shores. French-speaking men and women cleared the land and tended their crops. They raised large families and lived in peace with their neighbours, the Micmac Indians.

Forgotten by France and ignored by Quebec, the farmers lived by their own rules. They became a unique new people—the Acadians.

"Acadian Farms" by Dusan Kadlec.

HOW THEY LIVED

Jeanne pushed open the heavy wooden door that led into her home. In her arms, she held two large round loaves of bread. The bread smelt warm and inviting in the crisp autumn air. It was fresh from the outdoor stone oven that Jeanne's family shared with their neighbours.

Jeanne had spent all her 12 years in Acadia. Her parents had come from France long before she was born. They had built their fine stone house with their own hands.

As Jeanne put the brown loaves on the table, she heard her baby sister give a small cry. Jeanne gently rocked the cradle until the baby was quiet. Across the room, her two little brothers played with the wood in front of the fire. The firelight danced and licked the bottoms of the iron pots that hung over the hearth.

Maman stood by the big wooden table, humming a tune while she chopped turnips. Two wild geese hung from the rafter, waiting to be plucked. There was always so much work to do, thought Jeanne. Always water to fetch, weeds to pull, dinners to cook, floors to scrub. . . .

"Little one," said Maman, jolting her out of her thoughts. "If Marie is asleep, come help with the supper."

Jeanne got up and dreamily fetched a knife. As she chopped the turnips into small pieces, she smelt a lovely aroma from the fire. It was the pork, browning in the large black pot. Soon Maman would add turnips, cabbage, and water to make Jeanne's favourite soup. Maman had grown herbs last summer, so she would also add rosemary and thyme.

When Jeanne finished cutting up turnips, she began to chop apples. These were wild apples that Jeanne had found herself near the stream the day before. Maman would cook them with maple syrup and cinnamon sprinkled on top.

Jeanne remembered how the sugar had been boiled from maple sap in the spring. It had been kept fresh in the dark, cool root cellar beneath the floor. The cinnamon had come from France in a great sailing ship. The ship brought many good things, like lemons and molasses. While supper was cooking, Maman sat down for a few minutes at her spinning wheel. Jeanne set the table and watched her mother deftly twist the rough wool into yarn. Maman was planning to weave a big bright cover for the large bed in the sleeping loft.

Jeanne thought her mother looked very tired. She knew another baby was coming the next spring. Maman never complained though, no matter how much work there was. Once, Jeanne had asked her if she might be happier in France. Maman had just laughed and said that here she was free to live as she chose.

Jeanne fetched the butter and cut the bread into thick dark slices. Soon her father would be home from his hard work in the fields. Maman would greet him with a warm smile that would lift the cares from his heart. Then she would serve him a fine meal, fit for the king of France.

An Embattled Leader

Charles de La Tour loved Acadia, with its fertile valleys and rocky, fogbound coasts. For most of his life, he struggled to control its lands.

La Tour first came to Acadia in 1610, when he was only 17. He settled at Port Royal with his father to help *Jean de Poutrincourt* build his colony.

1 In 1613, the English raided Port Royal and burned it to the ground. La Tour and others took to the forests and lived with the Micmac Indians. La Tour became a fur trader and helped govern the remnants of the French colony.

2 When La Tour grew older he became the leader of the French in Acadia. He built Fort La Tour, a strong trading fort at the southern tip of Nova Scotia. In 1627, war broke out between England and France. All of New France fell to the English except Fort La Tour.

3 In 1632, the French regained Acadia. La Tour was forced to share control with a governor appointed by France. He moved his headquarters to Fort Sainte-Marie, at the mouth of the Saint John River.

4 In 1635, Charles D'Aulnay was appointed the new French governor. D'Aulnay and La Tour soon began to struggle for control of Acadia. They attacked one another's forts and called each other traitors.

6 With his wife dead and his lands gone, La Tour went to Quebec. When D'Aulnay drowned in 1650, La Tour returned to Acadia as governor. He married D'Aulnay's widow, Jeanne, to seal the peace between them.

7 La Tour was governor for a year when the British captured Acadia. He went to England as a prisoner, then returned to Acadia as a fur trader. In 1656, he retired with Jeanne to Fort La Tour. There he settled down happily to enjoy the land he loved.

5 In 1640, La Tour married *Marie*, a strong, gallant woman who supported his struggle. In 1645, while La Tour was away, D'Aulnay attacked his headquarters. Marie fought bravely, but was at last forced to surrender. She died three weeks later, broken-hearted at the defeat.

Heroine of Acadia

In 1640, Marie left Paris to marry *Charles de La Tour*. She went to live at Fort Sainte-Marie, at the mouth of the Saint John River. At that time, La Tour was fighting with Charles D'Aulnay for control of Acadia.

In 1645, La Tour left home to find support for his struggle in Boston. Marie stayed behind with a few dozen men to defend the fort. Here is the story of the battle that followed, as one of D'Aulnay's men might have told it.

"I still remember my first view of Madame La Tour. She looked down at our ships from the tower of her fort, the sun shining on her helmet and breastplate. She looked like a great warrior queen from days of old.

"Under D'Aulnay's orders, we began to bombard her fort with our cannons. We had over 200 men, and Madame had less than 50. Yet she kept up such a storm of shells, that I felt sure our ships would sink.

"After three days, Madame's fort began to weaken at last. A hole appeared in its wooden walls, then another. Some of our men reached the shore, dragging their cannons behind them. Madame rallied her men and drove our gunners back.

"The fourth day was Easter Sunday. There was a lull in the fighting, and both sides took the chance to rest. Later I learned Madame went to the chapel to say her Easter prayers.

"Suddenly the news began to spread through our ships. D'Aulnay had bought off Madame's sentry! Quickly, we climbed into small boats and rowed to shore. Then, silently, we scaled the walls of the fort.

"The Fate of the Defendants of Fort LaTour." Marie died in prison three weeks after witnessing the deaths of her men. Some say she died of a broken heart. Others say D'Aulnay poisoned her.

"By the time the alarm was raised, most of us were inside. Madame raced toward us at the head of her men, holding her sword high. 'Courage!' she cried, and the men behind her cheered.

"We fought hand to hand, and the battle raged for hours. Swords clanged against swords, and spears against spears. Madame fought bravely, but she could not win. We outnumbered her men by four to one.

"At last, D'Aulnay called a stop to the fighting. 'We've beaten you!' he roared. "Surrender, and I'll spare all your men!'

Slowly Madame nodded and laid down her sword in defeat. One after another, her men dropped their swords and spears on the floor.

"I'll never forgive D'Aulnay for what happened next. Suddenly, he began to rage and storm like a madman. He cursed Madame and swore he would kill every last man who had fought against him.

"D'Aulnay picked one of Madame's men to act as hangman. Then he made a noose of thick rope and placed it around Madame's neck. With tears in her eyes, she pleaded with D'Aulnay, not for herself but for her men.

"As we watched in horror, D'Aulnay's hangman killed Madame's soldiers one by one. When it was over, D'Aulnay cut Madame loose and took her prisoner. He took her to Port Royal and threw her into his dungeon. She died three weeks later, sick and broken-hearted."

New Brunswickers say that on a foggy day they can see the ghost of Marie de La Tour. She patrols the site of her old fort near Saint John harbour. She walks slowly and sadly, her long grey gown fading into the mists of Fundy Bay.

The Unlucky Acadian

Nicolas Denys was not a lucky man. All his schemes seemed doomed to end in ruin and disaster. Yet, through all his trials, Denys never stopped hoping for success.

In 1634, Denys started Acadia's first lumber business. The next year, Charles D'Aulnay became governor of the colony. D'Aulnay forbade Denys to export his lumber to France.

Around 1645, Denys built a fishing and trading post in present-day New Brunswick. Two years later, D'Aulnay seized the post and forced Denys to leave Acadia.

After D'Aulnay died, Denys built two more fishing posts on Cape Breton Island. D'Aulnay's widow sent soldiers to seize the posts and throw Denys into jail. When he was free, he set up his business again. This time, he was ambushed by a rival merchant and thrown into a dungeon at Port Royal.

After Denys was freed, he started a fishing and farming colony on the Nova Scotia coast. He soon fell deeply into debt and rival traders attacked his settlement. Denys moved his family to Cape Breton Island and built a trading post.

In 1668, the Cape Breton trading post burned down. Denys lost everything, including his home and furniture. Broken-hearted, he returned to his trading post in New Brunswick.

Now, at age 70, Denys became an author. He wrote a lively account of life in Acadia and it was published in Paris. In this book, Denys wrote that his life had been "thwarted by a thousand misfortunes." However, the unlucky Acadian could still look on the bright side. "I believe," he wrote, "I have not altogether lost my time."

Chapter Three

THE GREAT DAYS OF NEW FRANCE
1663 - 1763

For God and King
Marguerite Bourgeoys
Jean Talon
François de Laval
Habitants of New France
Pierre Radisson

The Days of Frontenac
Madeleine d'Allonne
Count Frontenac
Robert de La Salle
Madeleine de Verchères
Kateri Tekakwitha
Henry Kelsey

The Colony at Peace
Michel Sarrazin
Thanadelthur
Pierre de la Vérendrye
Eunice Williams
Noël Levasseur

The Expulsion of the Acadians
Paul Mascarene
Charles de Boishébert
Jean-Louis Le Loutre

The Fall of New France
Louis-Joseph de Montcalm
James Wolfe
Robert Stobo

FOR GOD AND KING

"The king regards his Canadian subjects... as his own children." With these words, in 1663, King Louis XIV took direct control of New France. He and his ministers began making changes to help the colony grow.

The king appointed three leaders to rule the colony for him. The intendant was the most powerful. He controlled the daily life of New France, including all legal and economic matters. The bishop ran the churches, schools, hospitals, and missions of the colony. The governor was in charge of relations with the Indians, and all military matters.

New France's first intendant was *Jean Talon*, a man of great energy and vision. He brought out hundreds of women settlers, known as the "filles du roi." He encouraged farmers to marry and raise large families. He built a lumber mill, a shipyard, and other industries so the colony could become self-supporting.

Under Talon, New France grew and thrived as never before. The settlers, or "habitants," rolled back the wilderness to clear new land for their farms. Under the seigneurial system, the settlers rented their land from "seigneurs," or landowners. They paid low rents—a small portion of their produce and a few days' work a year.

Talon also expanded the fur trade and sent explorers to find new lands. However, he was too late to stop two great explorers from leaving New France. *Pierre Radisson* and Médard des Groseilliers offered their services to the British. They built the first trading posts on Hudson Bay and started the Hudson's Bay Company.

"Reception of Intendant Talon by Monseigneur Laval." Between them, *Intendant Talon* and *Bishop Laval* controlled almost every aspect of life in New France. The governor usually ranked a poor third.

Mother of Ville-Marie

Marguerite Bourgeoys came to Ville-Marie (Montreal) in 1653. She was all ready to start the colony's first school. However, Ville-Marie had only one girl the right age to be taught! Marguerite changed her plans and helped the poor and sick.

In 1658, Marguerite started her school at last. She taught French and Indian girls in a cold, rundown stable. She taught them how to read and write, and how to cook, spin, and sew. As her school grew, Marguerite sent to France for other teachers.

Marguerite loved teaching, and cheerfully gave up her own comfort. She lived on bread and soup, and sometimes even gave these meals away. Often she set out on horseback or snowshoes to teach children who lived far away.

In 1665, the first "filles du roi" arrived at Ville-Marie. These were young French women who had come to New France to find husbands.

Marguerite gave the girls a home and taught them pioneer skills. She put up a sign on her door —"Girls to Marry." Then she talked to each man who arrived, and helped him choose a wife. Many young couples named their first babies "Marguerite."

Over the next years, Marguerite went on working for the colony. She built new schools and started an order of teaching nuns. She helped the poor and took care of the sick. She watched over the colony like a kindly mother, full of wise advice and practical help.

In 1982, almost 300 years after her death, Marguerite Bourgeoys was declared a Roman Catholic saint. She was the first Canadian woman to receive that title.

This impression of Mother Bourgeoys was painted in 1920.

JEAN TALON   c. 1625–1694

The Great Intendant

> I have denied myself the pleasures of life. I sacrifice everything to my work.
>
> —Jean Talon

Jean Talon wore the fancy clothes of a man of fashion and leisure. His frilled shirts and plumed hats were misleading, however. Talon loved hard work with a passion, and he brimmed with energy and brilliant ideas.

In 1665, Talon went to New France as its first intendant. Right away, he set to work to make the colony grow. He sent for more settlers from France and gave them free grants of land.

Talon knew that a colony could not grow without women. New France had only 1 single female for every 15 single men. Talon asked France to send him hundreds of healthy young women to marry his settlers. These were the "filles du roi," or "daughters of the king."

During the next seven years, over 1000 filles du roi landed in New France. Talon made sure nearly all of them found husbands. He took away fishing and hunting rights from any bachelor who refused to get married!

"The Coming of the Filles du Roi." For his young colony, Talon wanted only marriageable women who were "strong, healthy and free from natural blemish."

"Canada's First Shipyard." Under Talon's energetic leadership, New France blossomed in a brief golden age.

Once the settlers were married, Talon wanted them to have lots of children and grandchildren. He gave large grants to fathers with 10 children or more. He fined parents whose daughters were not married by age 16, or sons by age 20.

Talon travelled all over New France by canoe and on horseback. He visited even the most isolated settlers to find ways to help them. When he found they needed livestock, he sent to France for cattle, sheep, and horses. He also gave out tools and seed.

Talon wanted the settlers to provide for all their own needs. He imported looms so the women could spin wool and weave cloth. He started a shoe factory and even a hat factory! He wrote proudly to the king that he had "all that I need to clothe myself from head to foot."

Under Talon, New France grew as never before. He expanded fishing and lumbering in the colony, and started many new industries. He built New France's first sawmill, brewery, tannery, coal mine, and shipyard.

Talon also greatly expanded the fur trade. He sent out traders to explore lands from Hudson Bay to the Mississippi. Soon France extended its claim to more than three-fourths of all North America.

In 1672, Talon left New France because of poor health. In only seven years, he had more than doubled the number of settlers in the colony. King Louis XIV made Talon a count and appointed him his personal secretary.

Talon retired in 1692 and lived quietly until his death. He never raised a family of his own. The man who forced so many bachelors to marry stayed single all his life.

FRANCOIS DE LAVAL   1623–1708

First Bishop of Quebec

As a young man, François de Laval dreamed of a simple life as a missionary. He became a Jesuit priest and rose quickly in the Catholic Church. In 1658, he was made a bishop. The next year, he set sail to lead the Church in New France.

2 In late 1659, an epidemic of sickness swept through Quebec. Laval worked day and night to care for the sick. He helped any way he could, even by making beds.

3 Laval worked hard to increase the power of the Catholic Church in New France. He brought more priests from France and sent more missionaries to work among the Indians.

4 In 1663, Laval started the Seminary of Quebec to train priests. This later became Laval University. Laval also started other schools, including one for woodcarvers and other craftsmen.

1 Laval lived by strict rules of piety. He slept on a hard bed, ate simple food, and gave most of his money to the poor. Although he was a bishop, he chose to live in poverty.

5 Laval lived a holy life and expected others to do the same. He frowned on parties, games, makeup, and pretty clothes. Girls could dance only with girls, and only if their mothers were present.

6 In 1674, Laval became the first Bishop of Quebec. Laval tried to use his power to stop the use of liquor in the fur trade. After a long fight with *Governor Frontenac*, he was forced to admit defeat.

7 Laval retired in 1688, after his health gave out. He spent his last years living quietly in Quebec. Before he died, he gave away all he owned. He even shared his last frugal meals with the hungry.

HOW THEY LIVED

Jacques looked anxiously up at the sky. Grey thunder clouds were gathering over the river. He would have to work faster to get the hay in before the rains came to spoil it.

It was a still, sultry day in late August. Jacques' father worked up ahead, cutting the hay with swift, sure strokes of his scythe. His mother followed behind, turning the hay over with her wooden pitchfork to dry. Jacques and his younger sister, Annette, loaded the dry hay onto an ox-cart.

The Bouchards had been haying now for almost a week. This was their last field. Jacques hardly noticed the heat any more, or the prickly dust from the newly-cut hay. His muscles had grown hard from the long days of work.

"I wish it *would* rain," grumbled Annette beside him. She had stopped to swat a deerfly that had landed on her arm. "My clothes are all sticking to me in the heat."

Jacques ruffled her hair fondly. Annette was only ten, not old enough really for such hard work. "If it rains, the hay will grow mouldy," he said. "Then our horse and oxen will have nothing to eat in the winter."

"I wish Claude were here," Annette complained. "Why does he have to work for Seigneur Peronne today of all days?"

Secretly, Jacques also wished his older brother were here to help. However, for four days a year, the Bouchards had to work for the seigneur who owned their land. These days were always at busy times, like haying or harvest.

Jacques looked again at the sky. The clouds were much darker now. He began working faster, tossing the hay up over his shoulder onto the cart. Annette jumped up to spread the hay evenly on the cart as it landed.

Up ahead, Jacques' father stopped cutting. He began helping Maman turn the hay and gather it into piles for easy loading. Jacques urged the oxen forward. In the distance, thunder rumbled and lightning split the sky.

"Come on, Annette," cried Jacques, tossing her a pitchfork. "Hurry, or we'll lose the hay."

Jacques and Annette threw themselves into their work, oblivious now to the heat and the buzzing flies. They moved forward down the row of cut hay, slowly but surely loading it onto the cart. Papa and Maman dropped back to help, and together the Bouchards raced against time.

At last, only a few piles of hay were left to load. As Jacques bent down with his pitchfork, he felt the first large raindrops splash against his arm.

"Leave that!" yelled Papa. "Let's get this load to the barn!"

Papa tugged on the yoke to hurry the oxen. Jacques pushed the cart from behind, and Maman walked alongside to steady the load. Annette ran ahead to open the barn doors wide.

Lightning flashed and thunder roared. As the Bouchards reached the barn, the skies seemed to open. Jacques hung back, letting the cool rain drench his aching body. Suddenly he felt very happy. The hay was in, and the long days of work were finally over.

Founder of a Fur-Trade Empire

When Pierre Radisson was about 11, he was captured by Mohawk Indians. A Mohawk family adopted him and gave him the name "Oninga." Radisson learned to hunt and fish, and he dressed in buckskin and furs.

After two years, Radisson escaped and went back to his life at Trois Rivières. There he met his sister's husband, Médard des Groseilliers. In 1659, the two men set off together as partners in the fur trade. They did not wait to get a trading licence from the governor.

Radisson and Groseilliers travelled far inland, past the western end of Lake Superior. The Sioux Indians told them of a "great store of beaver" farther north toward Hudson Bay. Perhaps these lands could be reached from Europe by sailing right into the Bay.

Radisson and Groseilliers returned to Trois Rivières with over 100 canoes laden with furs. They expected a great welcome in New France. The Iroquois had almost stopped the French fur trade, and the colony badly needed furs.

Instead of being welcomed, however, the two fur traders were treated like criminals. They were fined heavily for trading without a licence. Most of their furs were taken from them, and Groseilliers was even thrown into jail.

Radisson and Groseilliers were furious. They decided that, from now on, they would deal with the British instead of the French. They would open up a fur trade on the shores of Hudson Bay and send furs directly to England.

The two fur traders went to Britain to find support for their plan. Radisson dressed up like an Indian chief to meet the king. He told wild stories about the Hudson Bay lands and the vast riches awaiting them in furs. The king was amused and agreed to give his support.

In 1668, Radisson and Groseilliers set sail from Britain for the shores of Hudson Bay. Radisson's ship was forced to turn back, but Groseilliers' landed on the shores of James Bay. He loaded his ship with furs and sailed back to England.

The British were delighted with Groseilliers' cargo. In 1670, they started the Hudson's Bay Company. The Company took control of all the lands drained by rivers flowing into Hudson Bay. No one knew how vast an empire this would be.

After a while, Radisson forgave the French and agreed to work for them again. He built Fort Bourbon, the first French trading post on Hudson Bay. He also captured a New England ship that had been smuggling furs on the Bay.

Once more, however, the French treated Radisson unfairly. The governor took away his furs and returned the ship to its owners.

For the second time, Radisson left New France. He took the post of chief factor with the Hudson's Bay Company. He captured Fort Bourbon, which was soon renamed York Factory.

Radisson never returned to New France. He spent his last years on his country estate in England. The man who was raised by Mohawks ended his life as an English country gentleman.

"Radisson and Groseilliers" by Frederic Remington. Radisson is the young man standing in the canoe.

DAYS OF FRONTENAC

In 1672, *Count Frontenac* arrived in New France as its governor. Frontenac was a vain, quarrelsome man, who played favourites and made enemies. He was also a strong, dynamic leader.

Frontenac wanted to strengthen the fur trade and extend the borders of New France. He built Fort Frontenac (now Kingston) to give the colony a stronghold on Lake Ontario. He encouraged *Robert La Salle* and others to explore and claim vast new lands. Under Frontenac's leadership, New France stretched from the Gulf of St. Lawrence down to the Gulf of Mexico.

In 1682, Frontenac's quarrels got out of hand. He was recalled and replaced by another governor. Around this time, the British and Iroquois stepped up their attacks on New France. First one governor, then another, was unable to protect the colony.

In 1689, Frontenac became governor for the second time. He decided to strike directly at the enemies of New France. He sent raiding parties into New England settlements, and burned down Iroquois villages. He brilliantly defended Quebec against a strong British attack.

Frontenac's leadership at last won peace for the troubled colony. The Iroquois could see that New France was growing stronger. Meanwhile, their own numbers were dwindling from warfare and disease.

In 1701, the Iroquois made a lasting peace with the French. The Indians promised not to interfere while Britain and France struggled over the control of North America.

"Frontenac at Cataraqui." *Frontenac* hoped to impress the Iroquois with a show of French strength at Cataraqui. He ordered his men to build Fort Frontenac and finish it within four days.

MADELEINE D'ALLONNE   c. 1646–1718

Landowner and Fur Trader

Madeleine d'Allonne was a spirited woman, who liked the freedom of life in New France. She was one of the first women to settle at Fort Frontenac (now Kingston, Ontario). She became a friend of its leader, *Robert La Salle*, and may have been engaged to marry him.

1 Madeleine took charge of a large seigneury and played an active part in the fur trade. She lent money to La Salle and bid him farewell on his journeys of exploration.

2 In 1687, Madeleine heard that La Salle had been murdered. A few months later, she was almost killed herself. She was captured by Iroquois warriors and held prisoner for almost a year.

3 After her release, Madeleine found that her seigneury had been claimed for the fur trade. She went to Montreal and tried to regain her lands. She spent the rest of her life there, arguing tirelessly for the rights of settlers over fur traders.

Defender of Quebec

As a young officer, Louis Buade, Count Frontenac cut a dashing figure. He fell in love with Anne de La Grange, a haughty 16-year-old beauty. Anne's father forced her to enter a convent to keep Frontenac away. When he found out the couple were already married, he cut Anne out of his will.

Frontenac and Anne were almost penniless, but they both enjoyed luxury. As the years passed, they borrowed millions of dollars. Then, to avoid paying it back, Frontenac left Anne and went to New France as governor.

Frontenac arrived at Quebec in 1672. He wanted to rule, in his words, as a "high and mighty lord." He soon made enemies of the colony's powerful intendant and bishop. Once, he even had the intendant's son thrown in jail.

Frontenac wanted to expand New France's fur trade to the west and south. He built Fort Frontenac (now Kingston), the first French settlement on Lake Ontario. This was the first in a chain of French trading posts to the west.

After ten years of feuds and quarrels, Frontenac was recalled to France. In his absence, Anne had managed to keep their creditors away. Soon, however, the couple were again hopelessly in debt.

In 1689, Frontenac returned to New France as governor. This time, he would be too busy for petty feuds. The British and the Iroquois had joined forces to destroy the colony.

"Frontenac on the way to Cataraqui." Frontenac always travelled in high style. He loved to dazzle onlookers with his brilliant uniforms and his splendidly dressed attendants.

"Frontenac Receiving the British Envoy demanding the Surrender of Quebec." The French blindfolded the British envoy and led him to Frontenac by a roundabout route. They wanted the envoy to think the fort was much larger than it really was.

Frontenac decided to strike quickly against the British. He ordered attacks on three New England settlements. He told his men to fight like the Iroquois, moving through the forest in small ambush parties.

The British responded with a large show of force. In 1690, they sent a fleet of heavily armed ships up the St. Lawrence. When they reached Quebec, the British commander sent a young officer ashore to demand surrender.

Frontenac received the envoy in a splendid room, surrounded by elegant French officers. When he heard the message, he drew himself up grandly. "I have no reply to make," he pronounced, "other than from the mouths of my cannon and muskets."

Frontenac was as good as his word. After a week, the British gave up their attack and returned to New England.

Frontenac next wanted to end the war with the Iroquois. In 1696, he led an attack deep into Iroquois lands. He was 74, and he had to be carried through the woods in a chair.

Frontenac's attack won New France the peace it so badly wanted. The Iroquois could see they were fighting a losing battle. They had lost half their people to disease and warfare, and could no longer afford war with the French.

Frontenac's deeds quickly became legends. His wife Anne, however, was not impressed. Over the years, her marriage had grown cold and distant.

When Frontenac died, his old warrior's heart was sent to Anne in Paris. She bitterly refused to accept the gift. "I do not want a dead heart," she said, "which did not belong to me when beating."

Explorer of the Mississippi

Robert de La Salle was a hot-tempered, restless young man. He came to New France when he was 24, eager for fame and glory. He joined the fur trade and began to explore the lands west of Montreal.

2 At Niagara, La Salle built a 45-tonne ship called the *Griffon*. In 1679, he launched the ship on Lake Erie above Niagara Falls. The *Griffon* was the first ship to sail on the Great Lakes. A few months later, when La Salle was elsewhere, it mysteriously vanished.

3 In December 1681, La Salle set out to explore the Mississippi to its mouth. The river had been discovered earlier by another Frenchman, Louis Jolliet. La Salle set a fast pace and made good speed through the bitter winter months.

1 La Salle took charge of Fort Frontenac (now Kingston, Ontario). He rebuilt the fort and used it to control the Great Lakes fur trade. He soon journeyed west to build new forts and expand the trading empire of New France.

4 La Salle reached the Mississippi in February and launched his canoes amid breaking ice. In early March, he passed the place where Jolliet had turned back. La Salle and his men pushed on for another 1100 kilometers.

5 On April 6, La Salle reached the mouth of the Mississippi River. He claimed the land for France and named it Louisiana, in honour of King Louis XIV.

6 In 1684, La Salle set out to start a colony on the Mississippi. He sailed into the Gulf of Mexico, but landed too far west. For the next two years, he struggled to find his way back to the river.

7 In 1687, La Salle and 16 men walked north to find a way home. La Salle drove his men hard and lost his temper often. After two months, the men were starving and exhausted. They turned against La Salle and shot him dead.

Heroine of New France

"Madeleine" by Gerald Hayward, 1915.

On October 22, 1692, the seigneury at Verchères was attacked by an Iroquois raiding party. The seigneur and his wife were away from home. Their 14-year-old daughter, Madeleine, was working with the settlers in the fields. Here is a version of her story.

"It was a frosty morning, and we were working to get in the last of the harvest. My mind was far from my work. I was thinking of Papa, and hoping he would come home soon.

"Nobody heard the Iroquois warriors as they moved through the woods toward us. They must have stood watching us, waiting no more than 20 metres away.

"Suddenly, all chaos broke loose. The Iroquois seemed to fly toward us from the trees. Some of our settlers were killed at once, and others were taken as prisoners.

"The warriors didn't notice me at first, perhaps because I'm so small. I began to run toward the fort as fast as I could. Then one of the Iroquois saw me and gave chase.

"I ran faster than ever before, faster than I thought possible. My blood ran cold as I felt the Iroquois' hand close down on my shoulder. With all my strength, I struggled away and left him grasping my neckerchief. I almost cried with relief when I heard the gates of the fort slam shut behind me.

"My relief didn't last long, though. Soon the fort was surrounded by Iroquois warriors. The only people left inside were two soldiers, my little brothers, an old man of 80, and me! I didn't know what to do. I knew the six of us couldn't hold out for long.

"By this time, the Iroquois were at the gates. I fired a cannon to drive them back from us. I hoped another settlement might hear, though I knew help would take days to reach us. How could so few of us fight off so many?

"Then I realized something. The Iroquois didn't know there were only six of us. If we made a great commotion, maybe we could trick them. We could make them think there were dozens of soldiers in the fort!

"I put on a soldier's hat and we all rushed about, singing and shouting. We banged pots and pans together, and fired rifles from different places around the walls. You can't imagine how much noise six people can make if their lives depend on it! We were soon hoarse and exhausted, but somehow we kept going.

"The plan worked! The Iroquois kept up their seige for days, but they never launched a big attack. We hardly slept at all, but we kept them at bay until the soldiers came from Montreal."

Madeleine saved the fort at Verchères and the lives of all inside. Later, in 1722, she proved her bravery once more. She saved the life of her husband, Pierre, during a fight with two drunken men.

"The Iroquois Attack of Fort Verchères." Notice that this painting shows another version of Madeleine's story. She still wears a kerchief around her neck, and there are two women present in the fort.

KATERI TEKAKWITHA   1656–1680

The Lily of the Mohawks

When Kateri was four, a plague of smallpox swept through the longhouses of her village. Kateri's parents died and she became very ill for a long time. She grew well again, but the smallpox left her face scarred and her eyes weak.

Kateri went to live with her aunt and uncle, who were leaders in her village. As she grew older, she felt drawn to the teachings of the Catholic religion. Her uncle disapproved of this new interest. He wanted her to get married and remain true to the beliefs of her people.

Kateri followed the longings of her own heart. When she was 19, she was baptized a Christian. After this, her friends and family turned against her. She left her village and took refuge in a Jesuit mission near Montreal.

Kateri was a kind young woman with a pure heart and a warm smile. She found great happiness in helping others and cheerfully sacrificed her own comfort. When she was alone, she prayed at an altar that she built herself.

Kateri did not give up all her Indian ways. She dressed in buckskin and went on winter hunting trips with her people. She became known as the "Lily of the Mohawks."

Kateri never grew very strong after her sickness. After years of fasting and hardship, her health broke down again. She died peacefully when she was only 24.

After Kateri died, people said that wonderful miracles occurred. Some said her face lost its scars and shone with a radiant beauty. Others said they

Kateri's portrait was done two years after her death. According to the artist, she appeared in a vision and asked for her portrait to be painted.

were cured of diseases after they prayed for her help.

In 1980, the Catholic Church declared that Kateri was "among the blessed in heaven." Someday she may become the first North American Indian to be named a saint.

HENRY KELSEY   c. 1667–1724

First Non-Native on the Prairies

This plain affords nothing but beast and grass
And over it in three days time we past
Getting into ye woods on the other side
It being about forty-sixe miles wide.
This wood is poplo ridges with small ponds
   of water.
There is beavour in abundance but no otter.

      —from Henry Kelsey's *Journal*

Luckily, Henry Kelsey was a better explorer than he was a poet. This verse from his journal describes his first visit to the Canadian Prairies. The vast plains were broken by "poplo" (poplar) ridges and "beavour" ponds.

Henry Kelsey joined the Hudson's Bay Company when he was 17. He went to York Factory and learned the basics of the fur trade. He made many friends among the Cree Indians and liked to go with them on their travels. His Cree friends called him Mitsah-paysish, or "Little Giant."

In 1689, Kelsey left York Factory to "invite the remoter Indians to a trade with us." He headed southwest from Hudson Bay for almost 1000 kilometres. He reached the land of the Assiniboines, and became the first non-Native to see Canada's Prairies.

Kelsey claimed the land for the Hudson's Bay Company, then pushed farther west. He saw great herds of buffalo and was attacked by huge grizzly bears. For two years, he wandered through the vast new lands. He opened up trade among the

"Kelsey on the Plains" by Rex Woods.

Indians and wrote poems about the wonders he saw.

Kelsey spent the next 30 years working for the Hudson's Bay Company. He became chief trader, then governor over all the posts at the Bay.

After Kelsey died, his journals vanished. They were found in Ireland more than 200 years later. The journals are now among Canada's treasures, bad rhymes and all.

THE COLONY AT PEACE

In 1713, France and Britain stopped their long war for control of North America. Both countries signed a peace settlement, the Treaty of Utrecht.

Under the treaty, Britain gained Newfoundland and Hudson Bay, and took control of most of Acadia. France kept its lands around the St. Lawrence and Great Lakes, and around the Mississippi. France also held onto present-day Cape Breton and Prince Edward Islands.

For the next 30 years, New France was free from war. At last its people could pursue the gentle arts of peace. *Michel Sarrazin* became the colony's first scientist, and made careful studies of its plants and animals. *Noël Levasseur* became New France's master woodcarver. He carved fine church altars and proud figureheads for the colony's ships.

During this time, the fur traders of New France pushed deep into the continent's interior. *Pierre La Vérendrye* built a chain of French trading posts that stretched west to present-day Winnipeg. His sons became the first non-Natives to see the foothills of the Rocky Mountains.

Meanwhile, the British also pushed into Canada's interior. British traders took control of the fur trade far west of Hudson Bay. They did this with the help of *Thanadelthur*, a Chipewyan woman who wanted to help her people.

"Bridge on the River La Puce" by Thomas Davies. This scene of country life in Quebec was not painted until 1790. However, it could easily have been painted 100 years earlier.

MICHEL SARRAZIN 1659–1734

Canada's First Scientist

Michel Sarrazin came to New France as a young doctor of 26. He was a quiet man who liked to spend time alone. He became fascinated by the strange plants and animals of the New World.

1 Sarrazin roamed the fields and woods of New France, risking many dangers. He studied hundreds of plants, and sent samples back to France. The common pitcher plant, which devours insects, was named *Sarracenia purpurea* in his honour.

2 Sarrazin also studied animal life, and made detailed reports on muskrats, beavers, and porcupines. He found one animal unpleasant to study—the "frightful" Canadian skunk.

3 Sarrazin was New France's only doctor for almost 50 years. He tended the colony through cruel epidemics, and caught many of his patients' diseases. He died of smallpox at age 75.

THANADELTHUR   d. 1717

Woman of Peace

The British traders called her Slave Woman. They found her, lost and starving in the frozen northern forests. She had escaped from the Cree after months in captivity as their slave.

Thanadelthur was a Chipewyan from the lands west of Hudson Bay. She had grown up hating the terrible war between her people and the Cree. Unlike the Cree, the Chipewyans had no guns. The Cree warriors stopped them from taking their furs to the trading posts on Hudson Bay.

The British took Thanadelthur back with them to York Factory. She spent the winter there, learning to speak English. For a long time, the British had wanted to open up trade with the Chipewyans. They asked Thanadelthur to lead a peace-making mission to her people.

Thanadelthur set out in June with over 100 Cree and William Stuart, a British trader. In autumn, she crossed the Churchill River and headed into the barren lands. Many Cree fell ill, and food was very scarce.

When winter came, the peace party broke into small groups to survive. Bitter winds and raging blizzards tore across the barren lands. Food became impossible to find. Once, Thanadelthur and Stuart went eight days without a bite to eat.

Through all these hardships, Thanadelthur refused to turn back. She urged the small group forward, inspiring them with the strength of her will. As she walked, she searched the horizon endlessly for some sign of her people.

One day, Thanadelthur came across a horrible scene. Fighting had broken out between the Chipewyans and a Cree group. Many Chipewyans lay dead, their bodies frozen in the snow.

Thanadelthur's Cree followers were frightened. They thought the Chipewyans would blame them and kill them in revenge. Thanadelthur convinced Stuart and the Cree to wait for ten days. Then she set out alone to find her people.

After a long, lonely trek, Thanadelthur at last reached a Chipewyan camp. Over 400 warriors had gathered there to plan revenge on the Cree.

Thanadelthur drew a deep breath and launched herself into a long speech. She told the warriors of the long hard journey she had made to find them. She gave them gifts from the British traders, and told them of the fine goods they could buy with their furs.

For two days, Thanadelthur went on arguing and pleading for peace. Her throat became sore and her voice began to give out. She kept on talking, for she knew the fate of her people hung in the balance.

At last, on the third day, Thanadelthur broke through the Chipewyans' resistance. They agreed to return with her and discuss peace with their age-old enemies.

Exhausted and happy, Thanadelthur led her people back to Stuart and the Cree. She arrived there just in time, ten days exactly after she had left. With tears of joy, Thanadelthur watched as the Chipewyans and the Cree smoked the pipe of peace.

"A Chipewyan Woman Makes Peace with the Crees, 1715" by Franklin Arbuckle.

PIERRE DE LA VERENDRYE   1685–1749

Explorer of the West

Pierre de La Vérendrye was one of the first great explorers to be born in Canada. He joined the army when he was only 12, and later became a fur trader. In 1728, he took over the French trading posts north of Lake Superior.

2 In 1731, La Vérendrye set out to find the western sea. He took his three sons and his nephew. The group pushed westward from Lake Superior and reached Rainy Lake. They built a trading post, then continued their journey west.

1 La Vérendrye talked to the Indians who traded their furs at his posts. He learned of a chain of lakes and rivers stretching far to the west. He hoped these waters would lead to a great western sea emptying into the Pacific.

3 Over the next years, La Vérendrye worked hard to expand the fur trade. He built more posts to intercept furs before they reached the British at Hudson Bay.

4 La Vérendrye made many trips back to Montreal to raise support for his travels. Although he was greatly expanding the French fur trade, most of his requests for money were turned down.

6 In 1742, La Vérendrye sent his sons to explore further west. For many months, they roamed the plains. On New Year's Day 1743, they became the first non-Natives to see the foothills of the Rockies.

5 La Vérendrye pushed on westward, despite his lack of funds. He built fur-trading posts at present-day Winnipeg and Portage La Prairie. As he explored and traded, he kept on searching for a way to the western sea.

7 As the years passed, La Vérendrye found less and less support for his work. At last, he was forced to resign his command of the western posts. He returned to Montreal a disappointed man. He died there six years later.

An English Mohawk

Eunice Williams was born in New England, the daughter of a Puritan minister. She grew up in a sheltered, orderly home, and lived by the strict rules of the Puritan religion.

When Eunice was about eight, her life changed completely. A large force of French and Indians attacked her settlement. Eunice was captured by Mohawk warriors and taken north to New France.

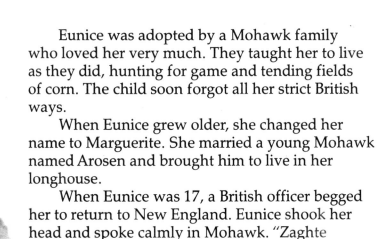

Eunice was adopted by a Mohawk family who loved her very much. They taught her to live as they did, hunting for game and tending fields of corn. The child soon forgot all her strict British ways.

When Eunice grew older, she changed her name to Marguerite. She married a young Mohawk named Arosen and brought him to live in her longhouse.

When Eunice was 17, a British officer begged her to return to New England. Eunice shook her head and spoke calmly in Mohawk. "Zaghte oghte," she said. "It may not be."

After many years, Eunice and Arosen took their children to visit Eunice's family. However, they refused to stay in her brother's large comfortable home. Instead, they camped in the orchard and entertained her family in their tent.

Eunice Williams lived to be nearly 90 years old. All that time, she remained true to her adopted Mohawk ways. She never showed any desire to return to her British way of life.

Master Woodcarver

When he was a boy, Noël played with the wooden chips in his father's workshop. As he grew older, he learned his father's trade of carpentry.

Noël had a special gift for carving wood into beautiful objects. He left his father's workshop to study with a fine wood sculptor from Paris. Soon Noël was at work carving altars and statues for the new churches of Quebec.

Noël's reputation quickly spread throughout New France. He created many fine works of religious art. He adorned altars with flying angels and statues of praying saints. He carved donkeys and oxen to stand in Christmas stables.

Noël did not only work for churches. He carved fine furniture and family coats of arms. He created richly-carved panels for town gates and governors' doors. He sculpted powerful figure-heads for the prows of New France's ships.

When Noël was 23, he settled at Quebec with his young wife Marie-Madeleine. Over the next years, the couple had 13 children. Noël taught some of his sons the art of woodcarving.

To Noël's delight, two of his sons were eager to learn all he could teach them. François-Noël and Jean Baptiste-Antoine became master woodcarvers in their own right.

After Noël died, his sons took over his studio. They went on carving beautiful works of art, just as he had taught them.

"Ange" by Noël Levasseur.

THE EXPULSION OF THE ACADIANS

In 1713, Britain took control of most of Acadia. Almost all the settlers chose to stay on their farms under British rule. By now, their roots in the land had grown deep.

Britain wanted the Acadians to swear oaths of loyalty to the British king. Most of the settlers refused. They did not want to fight against France, or to risk losing their Catholic religion.

In 1744, fighting broke out in Acadia. The British captured Louisbourg, the French fortress on Cape Breton Island. When Louisbourg was returned to France, the British began work on their own Atlantic fortress-town of Halifax.

In 1754, Britain and France once again drew close to war. The British worried more than ever about the loyalty of the Acadians. They came to a cruel decision. If the Acadians would not swear loyalty, they would have to leave their lands.

The next year, the Expulsion began. Acadians were forced from their homes at bayonet point and herded onto British ships. Their farms were burned down and their villages left in ruins. Husbands were separated from wives, and mothers from their children.

In all, nearly 10 000 Acadians were driven from their lands. Most were scattered in small groups among the British colonies to the south. Some escaped to the woods to fight against the British under *Charles de Boishébert*. Others found their way to the Mississippi lands, or began the long trek back to their ravaged homeland.

"The Dispersion of the Acadians" by Henri Beau. The tragic plight of the Acadians has inspired many works of art. Perhaps the greatest of these is the recent novel *Pélagie: The Return to a Homeland* by Antonine Maillet.

PAUL MASCARENE   c. 1684–1760

An Enlightened Governor

Paul Mascarene was born in France, but moved to England with his Protestant family. He joined the British army and took part in the 1710 capture of Acadia. In 1740, he took charge of Acadia's capital, Annapolis Royal.

2 In 1744, Britain and France were again at war. Mascarene defended Annapolis Royal against two attacks by the French. Most Acadian settlers stayed neutral, partly through respect for Mascarene.

1 Mascarene felt great sympathy for Acadia's French-speaking settlers. He treated them fairly in the courts and did not interfere with their Catholic religion. He hoped that someday they would become loyal British subjects.

3 After the war, Mascarene went on trying to win Acadian loyalty. He argued against those who spoke of driving the settlers from their lands. He retired in 1751, only four years before the Expulsion.

Defender of Acadia

Charles de Boishébert first went to Acadia from Quebec as a young soldier of 19. Over the next years, he fought many battles to protect French settlements from the British. In 1754, he took command of Fort La Tour on the Saint John River. When the British captured the fort, Boishébert escaped, disguised as a settler.

In 1755, the British forced thousands of Acadians to leave their lands. Boishébert took to the woods and led the settlers in resistance. Here is his story, as one of his followers might have told it.

"Our people are farmers, not fighters. Most of us come from farms that our families have owned for more than 100 years. All we wanted was to be left alone to work our land in peace.

"Then the British came. They wanted us to swear loyalty to their king, perhaps even to fight other Frenchmen. Our priests told us to refuse, and we obeyed.

"My village is called Petitcodiac. In September 1755, we heard the British were on their way to attack us. They planned to destroy our village and burn our farms. Then they would herd us like cattle onto ships and send us far from our homes.

"By September 3, the British were almost upon us. Then suddenly, like a miracle, help arrived. A young officer, Charles de Boishébert, came out of the woods to save us. He led a rough band of Micmac warriors and ragged Acadian farmboys.

"For the next two years, we ranged far and wide through Acadia's forests. We harassed the British until they did not dare to leave their forts. I learned to move silently in the woods like a Mic-mac warrior. I learned to strike without warning and take my enemy by surprise.

"As time passed, food became more scarce. Many farms had been burned, and crops were poor from those that remained. Boishébert had many hungry families to feed. He set up a refugee centre on the Miramichi and tried to build more farms there.

"I suppose, deep in our hearts, we knew we were doomed to failure. In 1758, Fort Louisbourg was taken by the British. Louisbourg was the last great French stronghold in Acadia. When it fell, all our hopes fell with it."

After the capture of Louisbourg, Boishébert left Acadia. He went to Quebec and fought with *General Montcalm* on the Plains of Abraham.

When Quebec fell, Boishébert returned to Acadia for one last visit. He found the Acadians hopelessly defeated. Boishébert sailed for France soon after, and stayed there the rest of his days.

"Boishébert was outnumbered, but he fought like a demon. The battle raged for three long hours. At last the British fled, leaving many dead behind them. Boishébert had lost only one man.

Boishébert asked the young men of our village to join his band of fighters. I agreed at once, and so did many others. Then Boishébert gathered up some of the poorest families from our district. He led us all back to the Saint John River, where other farmers had gathered for his protection.

French Leader in Acadia

Abbé Le Loutre came to Acadia when most of it was under British rule. He served as a missionary to the Micmacs and gradually his power grew. Under orders from France, he urged the Micmacs and Acadians to fight against their British rulers.

In 1749, Le Loutre moved to present-day New Brunswick where land was still claimed by France.

1 Le Loutre thought the British would force Acadians to renounce their Catholic faith. He forbade the Acadians to swear an oath of loyalty to Britain. He urged them to move their farms to land still claimed by France.

2 Most Acadians did not want to leave the farms their ancestors had built. Le Loutre grew angry and threatened to turn the Micmacs against them. He claimed the gates of heaven would be closed to those who disobeyed.

3 In 1755, the British expelled the Acadians from their lands. Le Loutre escaped to Quebec in disguise, but was later captured. He spent eight years in British jails before he was released. He spent the rest of his life helping exiled Acadians find new homes in France.

THE FALL OF NEW FRANCE

In 1756, Britain and France began their Seven Years War. This was to be their final struggle for control of North America.

In the first years of the war, the French forces held their own. Under their leader, *General Montcalm*, they captured British forts and defended their lands south of the Great Lakes.

In 1758, the tide began to turn. The British captured Fort Louisbourg, New France's stone fortress on the Atlantic. Then they attacked and captured other French forts, and took control of the Great Lakes.

In 1759, *General Wolfe* led a British attack on Quebec. In the dark of night, Wolfe's forces scaled the cliffs upriver from the town. The next morning, the French and British assembled their armies on the Plains of Abraham. After a short fierce battle, Quebec fell.

The next spring, British ships sailed up the St. Lawrence to seal the victory. In the fall, the French surrendered Montreal, their last stronghold on the St. Lawrence. The final battle was fought in 1762, at St. John's, Newfoundland.

The Seven Years War ended in 1763, with the signing of the Treaty of Paris. Under its terms, Britain took control of most of North America. France kept only the islands of St. Pierre and Miquelon to offer "shelter for French fishermen."

For 150 years, New France had been the setting for drama, glory, and adventure. Its people had suffered incredible hardships to make the wilderness their home. Now, after struggling through so many trials, New France ceased to exist.

"A View of the Taking of Quebec." According to one story, *Wolfe* found his path up the cliffs by watching some Quebec washerwomen. The women were carrying their laundry up a dry stream-bed from the river to the town.

The Homesick General

Louis-Joseph de Montcalm was not a soldier at heart. He loved the rolling hills and terraced vineyards of his home in southern France. He much preferred his tranquil fields to the musket-smoke and cannon-fire of war.

Montcalm became a soldier to uphold his family's long military tradition. He became an ensign at 9, and fought his first battle at 20. Over the next years, he fought in many wars and was wounded five times.

In 1749, Montcalm retired to his country estate. He spent seven happy years with his wife and young children. Then, in 1756, he was asked to command the French forces in North America. He wanted to refuse, but he agreed for the sake of his duty.

Montcalm sailed to New France and took quick action against the British. He led a force south of the Great Lakes to attack the British forts there. He captured Fort Oswego, and took over 16 000 British prisoners. The next year, he captured Fort William Henry, in present-day New York State.

Despite his success, Montcalm was unhappy in the rough colony. "I am deeply desirous of peace," he wrote his wife. "I think I should have given up all my honours to be back with you."

"Montcalm on the Plains of Abraham." Had Montcalm waited until help arrived, Canada's history might have been very different.

As time passed, Montcalm saw the tide of war turn against him. The British sent more troops and captured Fort Louisbourg on the Atlantic. Montcalm sent to Paris for more soldiers, but the French army was tied up in Europe.

In 1759, *General Wolfe* led the British up the St. Lawrence. He lay siege to Quebec, but Montcalm defended the city well. Then, in the middle of the night, Wolfe's men scaled the cliffs upriver of Quebec. By morning, they reached the Plains of Abraham, just outside the town.

If Montcalm had stayed behind Quebec's walls, he might have saved the day. Other French troops would have arrived to take Wolfe from behind. However, instead of waiting, Montcalm chose to attack.

Montcalm gathered his forces, most of them untrained settlers. Then he mounted his black charger and raised his sword up high. Slowly, he led his men forward into battle.

The British held their ground and fired one volley at the French. Montcalm watched as his lines collapsed in chaos. He swung his horse around and tried to rally his fleeing men.

"Death of Montcalm" by Justus Chevillet. Like most "Death of" paintings, this one is wildly inaccurate. Notice the palm trees and satin pillow. Montcalm actually died the morning after the battle at a house inside the city gates.

Suddenly, British grapeshot caught him in the abdomen and thigh. Montcalm managed to stay on his horse with help from his men. He painfully rode to the walls of the city and entered the Saint-Louis Gate.

When the townspeople saw their leader, they came running to his side. Women started to cry when they saw his wounds. "It is nothing, nothing at all," said Montcalm gallantly. "Do not grieve on my account, dear friends."

Montcalm died the next morning as dawn broke over the fallen town. He was buried in the Ursuline Convent, in a hole blasted by a British shell. His body rests there still, far from the fields and valleys of his beloved home.

The Conquering General

Up the River St. Lawrence our troops will
  advance!
To the Grenadiers' March we will teach them
  to dance!
Cape Breton we've taken, the next we will try
At their capital to give them another black eye!
And ye that love fighting will soon have
  enough!
Wolfe commands us, my boys, we shall give
  them hot stuff!

      —from "Hot Stuff," sung by Wolfe's soldiers

Wolfe at 13 is studying the history of a famous battle.

James Wolfe was a pale and sickly boy, but he had the heart of a lion. When he was 13, he volunteered to fight the Spanish with his father's regiment. By the time he was 18, he had fought many battles in distant lands.

In 1758, Wolfe fought in the British seige of Fort Louisbourg. He led a landing party through a storm of musket-fire to gain a British foothold on the shore. Then he led the left wing of the attack to a brilliant victory.

In June 1759, Wolfe sailed up the St. Lawrence to Quebec. He began firing his cannons at the town, but he knew this attack was useless. Quebec was surrounded by stone walls and perched atop high cliffs. As long as the French stayed inside, they would not be beaten.

As the summer passed, Wolfe looked for ways to draw the French into the open. He decided to attack upriver to cut off the French from supplies. He found a dry stream-bed that wound up the cliff-face two miles above Quebec.

The night of September 12 was cloudy and dark. Wolfe ordered some of his men to launch a noisy attack as a diversion. Then he and his ships slipped silently away.

At four in the morning, the first two dozen men climbed in pairs up the narrow path. At the top, they overpowered some French guards who were sleeping in their tents. Then 4000 Redcoats scaled the cliff, climbing two by two.

By morning, Wolfe's army was standing in battle-line formation on the Plains of Abraham. *General Montcalm* could scarcely believe his eyes. Rashly, he brought his own army forward to meet the attack.

As the French advanced, Wolfe ordered his front lines to kneel and hold their fire. The French came closer, firing wildly, but still Wolfe held his ground. Then, when the French were within 35 metres, he gave the order to fire.

Thousands of muskets roared at once, and dense white smoke filled the air. When it cleared, the French lines were in chaos. Hundreds of French lay dead or dying, and others were fleeing back to the town.

Wolfe led his men forward to rout the retreating army. In his brilliant red uniform, he made an easy target. He was shot in the wrist, but he scarcely seemed to notice. He bandaged the wound with his handkerchief and kept on.

Another bullet caught Wolfe in the stomach, then another full in the chest. He fell to the ground, mortally wounded. Two of his officers picked him up and carried him gently out of the line of fire.

As Wolfe lay dying, he gave his officers final orders for victory. His last words were those of a true soldier. "Now God be praised," he gasped. "Since I have conquered, I will die in peace."

"The Death of Wolfe" by Benjamin West. Very few of the people shown here were actually present at Wolfe's death. Some were "painted in" by the artist for a fee!

British Spy at Quebec

Robert Stobo was a young merchant from the British colony of Virginia. In 1755, he fought in a battle against the French for control of the Ohio Valley. The British lost, and Stobo was taken hostage by the French at Fort Duquesne.

1 Under the rules of war, hostages were not allowed to act as spies. Stobo decided to break this rule. He drew a map of Fort Duquesne and smuggled it out to the British.

2 Stobo was moved to Quebec and given the freedom of the town. Then, the next spring, the French found out about his map. He was convicted of spying and sentenced to the guillotine.

3 Stobo escaped in 1759 and joined the staff of *General Wolfe*. He led British raids against Quebec and told Wolfe all he knew about the surrounding countryside. Stobo may even have shown Wolfe his fateful path up to the Plains of Abraham.

Chapter Four

AFTER THE CONQUEST
1763 - 1812

A Broken Peace
James Murray
Pontiac—Obwandiyag
Sir Guy Carleton
Molly Brant—Degonwadonti
Pierre du Calvet

Two Canadas
John Graves Simcoe
Elizabeth Simcoe
Ezekiel Hart
Joseph Brant—Thayendenegea
François Baillairgé

Atlantic Lands
Joseph Des Barres
Mikak of Labrador
John Marrant
Newfoundland Settlers
Edward Winslow
Henry Alline

Pacific Shores
The Spanish Explorers
James Cook
Muquinna
George Vancouver

The Great Northwest
Peter Pond
Samuel Hearne
Matonabbee
Sir Alexander Mackenzie
English Chief

A BROKEN PEACE

After the Seven Years War, the British became rulers of much of North America. They now had to govern three very different groups of people. Over 1 500 000 English-speaking settlers lived in the East, mostly in the Thirteen Colonies. More than 60 000 French Canadians lived along or near the St. Lawrence River. Several tribes of Indians made their homes in the Ohio Valley lands of the West.

Trouble soon broke out in the Ohio Valley. Under *Chief Pontiac*, the western Indians rebelled against the loss of their lands. They won many early victories against the British, but eventually lost their war.

Meanwhile the British looked for ways to rule the French Canadians. First *James Murray*, then *Guy Carleton*, tried to treat them as fairly as possible. The Quebec Act of 1774 let French Canadians keep their language, religion, and customs.

The Quebec Act also extended Quebec's boundaries to include the Ohio Valley. This angered the people of the Thirteen Colonies, who wanted the Ohio lands for themselves. Many of the colonists had already begun to resent British rule. They viewed themselves as Americans, not British.

In 1775, the American Revolution began. The American rebels invited the people of Quebec to join their fight. When the French Canadians refused, the Americans attacked Montreal and Quebec City.

Montreal fell to the rebels, but Quebec City resisted a long American siege. When British ships arrived with help, the American rebels retreated southward. For the rest of the war, most of the fighting stayed in the south.

In 1783, the Thirteen Colonies gained their freedom from Britain. A new nation was born— the United States of America.

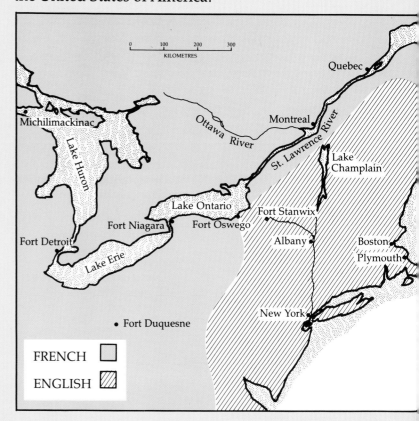

FRENCH AND ENGLISH FRONTIER, 1760

A Troubled Governor

James Murray came to North America as a British commander in the Seven Years War. He led a British brigade at the capture of Louisbourg, and he commanded the left flank of *Wolfe*'s attack on the Plains of Abraham.

In 1763, the Seven Years War ended. The British chose Murray to govern the huge new colony of Quebec. He would not find this easy to do.

2 Quebec's British merchants disliked Murray's tolerance of the French. The merchants took over the Assembly and tried to gain more power. To stop them, Murray decided to rule without an Assembly.

1 Murray told French Canadians they could keep their language, customs, and Roman Catholic religion. He made friends with Quebec's seigneurs and priests, and asked them to help govern their people.

3 The merchants complained to Britain, and Murray was charged with misrule. He faced trial in England, where a court dropped the charges against him. Although Murray remained Quebec's governor, he never returned to the troublesome colony.

War Chief of the Ottawas

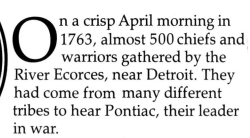

On a crisp April morning in 1763, almost 500 chiefs and warriors gathered by the River Ecorces, near Detroit. They had come from many different tribes to hear Pontiac, their leader in war.

Pontiac stood before the Indians in full battle-dress, his face painted for war. Eyes flashing with rage, he bitterly described how British soldiers had abused his people.

Since the fall of Quebec, the British had moved into the French forts and trading posts in the Ohio Valley. British traders paid less for furs, and often cheated Native traders. Unlike the French, the British refused to distribute much-needed supplies. The Indians had come to expect these gifts as payment for use of their lands.

Pontiac also spoke angrily of the many settlers who came each day from the British Colonies. Unlike the French, they seized land by force and treated the Indians with contempt. Before long, the British would destroy the Indian nations forever.

Pontiac outlined a daring plan of attack. During May, Indian war-parties would take each of the British forts by surprise. Then the Indians, along with the French, would take back the Ohio lands.

On May 1, Pontiac and 40 of his men arrived at Fort Detroit. They told Major Gladwin they had come to dance the Calumet, a dance of peace. As they danced, 10 sharp-eyed warriors slipped away to survey the fort. In this way, Pontiac learned all about Detroit's strengths and defences.

Pontiac did not learn, however, that Major Gladwin had a friend among the Indians. The day before the attack, Gladwin was somehow warned.

On May 7, Pontiac arrived at Fort Detroit with more than 300 warriors. He said he had come for a great council to discuss matters of importance. The gates swung open and the Indians marched in, clutching guns and tomahawks under their blankets.

In July 1766, Pontiac signed a treaty of peace. In this treaty, the British promised not to settle in the Indians' Ohio Valley lands. Pontiac did not live long enough to see the British government break their promise.

The next year, some warriors urged Pontiac to return to battle. He refused to break the treaty he had signed, and some of his followers turned against him. He was murdered in April 1769, at the hands of a Peoria Indian.

Pontiac and his men crossed the fort to the council-house where Gladwin was waiting. Inside the council-house, Gladwin watched closely as Pontiac spoke. Pontiac started to raise his wampum belt to signal his men to attack.

Quickly, Gladwin made a sign with his hand. All over the fort, British drums began to roll until the noise was almost deafening. Pontiac knew then he had been betrayed. He and his men quickly withdrew from the fort.

Although Pontiac's plan failed at Detroit, it was a great success elsewhere. Through May and June, all other forts west of Niagara fell to the Indians. However, the French never arrived with the help Pontiac had hoped for. Slowly the British regained their forts.

SIR GUY CARLETON 1724–1808

Soldier and Statesman

Guy Carleton first came to North America as an officer in the British army. The tall, gallant Irishman fought with *Wolfe* at Louisbourg. The next year, he was one of Wolfe's right-hand men at the siege of Quebec.

In 1766, Carleton became lieutenant-governor of the colony of Quebec. Two years later, he became governor.

2 On a trip to England, Carleton proposed to the daughter of the Earl of Effingham. She turned him down, but her younger sister did not. Lady Maria was 18 and Carleton was 48. They would eventually have 11 children.

1 Carleton knew that Britain needed the support of French Canada. He worked to protect the customs, language, and religion of French Canadians.

3 Carleton's ideas were behind the Quebec Act of 1774. The Act protected French Canadian rights and gave Quebec control of the Ohio lands. This angered American settlers and pushed them closer to rebellion. The next year, the American Revolution began.

4 Carleton was just leaving Montreal when American rebels captured the city. Disguised as an habitant, he escaped downriver in a small boat. He and a boatman called "Wild Pigeon" paddled silently with their hands.

5 On New Year's Eve, 1775, Carleton and his men defeated a major rebel attack. Later, Carleton was knighted for helping to save the colony.

6 After the war, Carleton made sure that Loyalists could leave the United States. He helped many to move north and find new homes in British North America.

7 In 1786, Carleton became governor-in-chief of all British North America. He found his lieutenant-governors hard to control, especially *John Simcoe*. Carleton retired in 1796, weary after his long service.

Matron of the Mohawks

The pretty Mohawk girl watched in the crowd as a young ensign rode across the assembly-ground. She caught his eye and laughed when he invited her to jump up behind him. Then, in a flash, she sprang onto the horse and spurred it into a gallop. Molly held on easily. Her eyes shone as her dark braids and blanket flew in the wind. Sir William Johnson never forgot the sight.

Molly Brant, or Degonwadonti, was born into a high-ranking Mohawk family. She and her younger brother, *Joseph*, spent much of their youth in New York's rich Mohawk Valley. The Mohawks were one of the Six Nations of the Iroquois Confederacy.

"Johnson Hall" by E.L. Henry. Molly helped her husband settle many British-Indian disputes. Over the years, she entertained thousands of Indian guests at Johnson Hall.

When she was 23, Molly married Sir William Johnson in a Mohawk ceremony. Sir William was Superintendent of Indian Affairs for most of British North America, and a special friend of the Mohawks. When he was dealing with the Indians, he lived as they did. During the Seven Years War, he convinced the Iroquois to trust the British.

Molly was kept busy as Sir William's wife. She bore nine children, managed a large estate, and looked after many guests. During a council to settle the *Pontiac* Rebellion, over 900 Indians stayed at Johnson Hall for several months.

Molly played a crucial role in Sir William's work. With her family's help, she gained support for her husband among the Iroquois. When Sir William was away, she took his place as adviser to the Mohawks. She earned the respect of the British as well as the Iroquois.

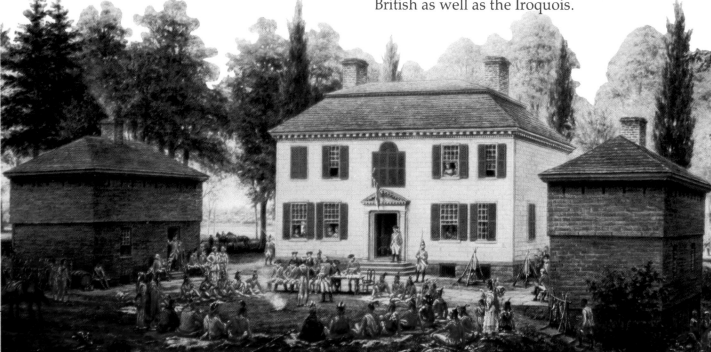

Sir William died in 1774, and other troubles soon followed. The American Revolution began, and the Johnson estates were seized. Molly retreated to a nearby Indian village.

Like her brother Joseph, Molly became a staunch Loyalist. She helped other Loyalists who had been driven into the woods. She also sent ammunition to those who fought with the British.

In August 1777, Molly learned that American soldiers were headed toward the British fort at Stanwix. She sent Indian runners to warn the British. As a result, the Americans were ambushed.

Molly's actions angered the Oneidas, the only one of the Six Nations that joined the American side. Molly was driven out of the Mohawk Valley. However, she persuaded other Iroquois tribes to stay loyal to the British.

Late in 1777, Molly joined the British forces at Fort Niagara. She worked tirelessly to smooth relations between the British and the Iroquois. She settled problems on both sides, and she advised the Iroquois on all important matters.

At the war's end, Molly moved to Cataraqui (now Kingston, Ontario). The Americans tried to lure her back to the Mohawk Valley with a large offer of money. Molly turned them down with scorn.

Molly stayed in Cataraqui and became a highly respected member of Upper Canada society. However, despite her high social position, she never abandoned the clothes or customs of the Mohawks.

The Unlucky Merchant

Pierre du Calvet was a merchant who lived in Montreal when the American rebels invaded. Here is a version of his story.

"Before the Americans captured Montreal, I was doing very well for myself. Business was good and I was a justice of the peace. *Governor Carleton* himself was godfather to my son, Guy.

"I still remember that day—November 12, 1775. I was at home when the explosions rattled my windows. Later they said I was getting ready to welcome the enemy. It wasn't true! Let me tell you, when my house was shaking I was as scared as anybody in Montreal!

"When the Americans finally got here, they were in bad shape. Lots of them had died along the way. I gave them supplies and they promised to pay me later. They would have taken what they needed anyway.

"By 1780 they still hadn't sent me any money. I wrote to the American government demanding to be paid. The British found my letters and accused me of siding with the Americans. They said I wanted money for spying, and they called me a traitor.

"Governor Haldimand (of Quebec) threw me in jail without a trial. I was kept there for almost three years. In May 1783, I was finally released. Then I sailed for England to plead my case there.

"That was two years ago, and Haldimand has still not answered for his crime against me. I may never get back what I have lost. My reputation is ruined forever."

Du Calvet never found the justice he was looking for. In 1786, on his way to England for the second time, he was lost at sea in a storm.

TWO CANADAS

The American Revolution had a dramatic effect on life in the colony of Quebec. Before the Revolution, the people there were almost all French. Then, after the Revolution, a great wave of Loyalist settlers changed the face of the province forever.

The Loyalists were settlers from the Thirteen Colonies who did not join in the American Revolution. Many of them escaped from the United States with only what they could carry.

Although Nova Scotia drew most of the Loyalists, thousands also poured into Quebec. Many moved west to the wild lands of present-day Ontario. Several thousand Iroquois Loyalists built homes there, along the banks of the Grand River.

The Loyalist settlers had struggled to remain British. The Quebec Act, which had protected the rights of the French, meant little to them. In 1791, a new act was passed to govern all the colonists, French and British.

The Canada Act of 1791 divided the huge colony of Quebec into two parts: Lower Canada and Upper Canada. Lower Canada kept French civil law and its seigneurial system. Upper Canada, where so many Loyalists had settled, would be governed by British law. Each province would have its own elected Assembly and its own lieutenant-governor. There would be two Canadas, each with its own language, laws, and religion.

"Circular Dance of the Canadians" by George Heriot. Life in the young colonies was not all hard work. There were evenings filled with music and dance at rough country homes and elegant balls.

First Governor of Upper Canada

In 1791, the vast province of Quebec was divided into Upper and Lower Canada. A British officer, John Graves Simcoe was chosen to become Upper Canada's first lieutenant-governor. He left England with his wife, *Elizabeth*, and two of their six children.

2 Simcoe planned to open Upper Canada's first parliament at Newark (now Niagara-on-the-Lake). When he got there, his house was not ready. He and his family moved into a two-room tent!

1 Simcoe was sworn in as lieutenant-governor at Kingston in July 1792. He insisted on as grand a ceremony as possible. Simcoe wanted life in Upper Canada to become "the very image" of life in Britain.

3 Simcoe's first parliament brought trial by jury and English law to the province. Other bills made plans for courthouses and jails, and made importing slaves illegal.

4 Simcoe founded the town of York (now Toronto) in 1793. At the naming ceremony, young Francis Simcoe was thrilled by the cannon-fire.

6 Simcoe had many roads built in Upper Canada. He wanted to attract settlers deep into the province, and to let troops move quickly in time of war. The longest new road, Yonge Street, ran north from York to Lake Simcoe.

5 Simcoe wanted to open up the western lands of the province. His generous land grants brought hordes of settlers from Britain and the United States. Some Loyalists were angry to see land given away to Americans.

7 Hard work and harsh conditions soon took their toll. Simcoe fell ill with headaches and fevers, and in 1796 he returned to England. In his short time as lieutenant-governor, the population of Upper Canada had almost tripled!

A Frontier Gentlewoman

Elizabeth Gwillim was 15 years old when *John Graves Simcoe* arrived at her family's home in Devon, England. John was 30 years old. He was a wounded war hero who had come to the country to regain his health.

When Elizabeth went riding and walking, John often kept her company. As time passed, the two fell in love. They married in December 1782, when Elizabeth was just 16.

Despite her youth, Elizabeth managed her household well. She and John lived in a 40-room mansion and gave many elegant parties. In the next nine years, Elizabeth became the mother of six children.

Elizabeth's life changed dramatically when John became lieutenant-governor of Upper Canada in 1791. The couple knew that Upper Canada was mostly unsettled wilderness. Sadly, they decided to leave their eldest four children in England with a family friend. They took the youngest two, who were still babies, with them.

After a short stay in Quebec City, Elizabeth and John travelled to Newark (now Niagara-on-the-Lake). Their house was not ready for them, so Elizabeth set up housekeeping in a tent. Newark became her home for the next two years. There she gave birth to a daughter, Katherine, who died in infancy.

"The Garrison at York" by Elizabeth Simcoe. Elizabeth loved to travel by canoe and sketch the passing scenery.

Despite her hardships, Elizabeth cheerfully faced the challenges of the frontier. She loved new experiences. Often she went on long rides and canoe trips with her husband. When she wrote to her children in England, she sent them sketches of the flowers and scenery.

Elizabeth's letters to England were written in the form of a diary. They give a vivid account of Canadian life in the late 1700s. Here are some examples:

March 19, 1794 — This is the month for making maple sugar. A hot sun and frosty nights cause the sap to flow most. Slits are cut in the bark of the trees and wooden troughs set under the tree into which the sap—a clear sweet water—runs.

February 19, 1796 — We dined in the woods on Major Shanks' farm lot where an arbour of hemlock pine was prepared, a band of music stationed near. We dined on large perch and venison. Jacob the Mohawk was there. He danced Scotch reels with more ease and grace than any person I ever saw, and had the air of a prince.

July 19, 1796 — This rapid (near Montreal) is much more frightful than the Long Sault. I cannot describe how terrifying the extent of furious dashing white waves appeared, and how the boat plunged and rose among them, the waves sometimes washing into the boat . . . .The men rowed with all their might and in passing it called out "Vive le Roy." We passed a rock which really seemed to fly from us.

The Simcoes returned to England after five years in Upper Canada. They took back a birchbark canoe, furs, and other wonderful presents for their family. Elizabeth lived to be 84 and spent the rest of her life in England. She never saw Canada again.

First Jewish Member of Government

In 1807, the people of Trois-Rivières gathered to hear the results of their elections. Ezekiel Hart had defeated Thomas Coffin to sit in Lower Canada's Legislative Assembly!

Ezekiel Hart was a popular lawyer from one of the town's leading families. His father, Aaron Hart, had come to Lower Canada with *General Wolfe*. He had been the first Jew to settle in the province.

Ezekiel had learned to take pride in the faith and customs of his people. As a lawyer, he never went to court on the Sabbath. He swore his legal oaths on the Old Testament instead of the Christian Bible.

When the Assembly opened, each of the new members came forward to swear an oath of office. When Hart's turn came, he explained that he would take his oath on the Old Testament. There was a stunned silence, then the Assembly burst into an uproar.

Hart's rival, Thomas Coffin, now saw his chance. He raised a petition asking for Hart to be thrown out of the Assembly. After all, even the British did not allow Jews to hold office. Coffin's petition was passed by the Assembly. In February 1808, Hart was told he could no longer sit in the legislature.

The people who had voted for Hart were furious. They wrote many angry letters to protest the Assembly's decision. They accused the Assembly of being backward and unjust. How dare it interfere with Trois-Rivières' right to choose its representative freely!

Another election was called for early May. On election day, Hart waited nervously in the courthouse while the votes were counted. The result was a great triumph! As the news spread, a brass band led a victory parade through the streets of Trois-Rivières. A group of soldiers hoisted Hart onto their shoulders and marched him to the town square to celebrate.

Unfortunately, Hart's triumph did not last long. The next time the Assembly met, it passed a law that no Jew could sit or vote in the legislature.

Hart ran for election a third time. He withdrew when he realized the Assembly would never allow him to join it. He retired from political life and devoted his time to his family and business.

Though Hart's own political career was over, he lived to see the triumph of his cause. In 1832, Lower Canada passed a law that gave the Jews the same rights as other Canadians. The law was introduced by Hart's own grandson, Benjamin. It was the first law in the British Empire to give equal rights to Jews.

War Chief and Statesman

Joseph Brant belonged to the Mohawk tribe, one of the Iroquois Six Nations. As a boy, he attended a British school and made powerful British friends. He became a leader among the Mohawks, and worked to protect their lands.

In 1775, the American Revolution broke out. The British asked Brant to support them against the Americans. Brant wanted to make sure the British would protect Iroquois land rights. He sailed to England to meet with King George III.

2 Brant travelled through Iroquois lands, urging his people to fight the Americans. Most of the tribes pledged their support. An Iroquois council named Brant "War Chief of the Six Nations."

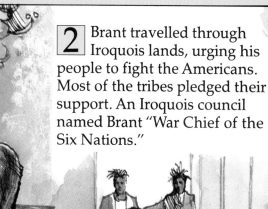

1 In England, Brant mixed easily with some of the country's most famous and powerful people. After talks with British leaders, he decided the Iroquois should keep their alliance with Britain.

3 Throughout the war, Brant led the Iroquois in raids against the American rebels. He always tried to protect women and children during his raids.

4 In 1779, the American rebels drove the Iroquois out of the Mohawk Valley. Thousands of homeless refugees poured into the British fort at Niagara. Brant fought on, determined to defeat those who had destroyed his homeland.

5 After the war, Britain handed over the Iroquois lands to the United States. Brant was furious, and felt his people had been betrayed. He protested bitterly and forced the British to compensate the Indians for their loss.

7 For the rest of his life, Brant worked tirelessly to help his people. He negotiated with the government for Indian rights, and imported European farming methods to help Iroquois farmers. He also helped the western Indians protect their land from American settlers.

6 Brant arranged for two grants of land to be set aside for the Mohawks. The largest was by the Grand River, between Lake Ontario and Lake Erie. Brant founded the village of Brant's Ford (now Brantford), with its own school, church, and flour mill.

125

Master Sculptor of Quebec

This may be a portrait of François Baillairgé or his son, Thomas.

François Baillairgé was born in 1759, the same year that Quebec fell to the British. He grew up in the hard years after the Conquest, when many French Canadians felt lost and defeated. As one of Quebec's finest artists, he helped bring French Canada's culture back to life.

Baillairgé first learned about art from his father, an architect and woodcarver. As a child, Baillairgé played happily in his father's workshop. When he was 19, he went to Paris to study sculpture and painting. He was the first Canadian sculptor to study in Europe.

When Baillairgé returned to Quebec City, he opened his own studio. His first big assignment was to decorate the inside of the Basilique, Quebec's beautiful new cathedral. His designs were highly praised, and soon his work was in great demand.

Baillairgé was a practical man who was proud of French Canada's long tradition of woodcarving. He created beautiful works of art, but he also made things for everyday use. He painted many store signs and family coats of arms. He even carved figureheads for the ships of Quebec.

"Figure on the Prow of the Schooner, *Royal Edward*" by François Baillairgé. Baillairgé may have used the sketch as a model for a figurehead he was carving.

Baillairgé designed many buildings and painted the portraits of Quebec's leading citizens. He was most famous, however, for his fine religious sculptures. His statues and carved altars adorned Quebec's many churches. Over the years, his work brought beauty into the lives of thousands.

Baillairgé was a true universal man, with many different interests. Besides painting and sculpture, he loved music, poetry, science, and history. He designed stage scenery for the theatre and served as an officer in Quebec's militia. In his later years, he even became Treasurer of Quebec City.

Baillairgé was Quebec's master sculptor, but others in his family were also talented. His brother, Pierre-Florent, carved many beautiful altars and church decorations. Baillairgé's son, Thomas, carried on the family work as a famous woodcarver and sculptor.

ATLANTIC LANDS

Slowly, wearily, the Loyalist woman carried her baby up the hill. When she reached the top, she turned to gaze out over the Bay of Fundy. Sadly she watched as her ship disappeared over the horizon. Later, she wrote:

> Such a feeling of loneliness came over me that, although I had not shed a tear through all the war, I sat down on the damp moss with my baby and cried.

After the American Revolution, almost 30 000 Loyalists came to Nova Scotia. These men and women had helped Britain in the war. They no longer felt safe in their old homes.

The first years in Nova Scotia were hard ones. There were food shortages and bitter winters. Many of the Loyalists had no idea how to live as pioneers.

Despite their hardships, however, most of the Loyalists stayed on. The land was surveyed and settled, and new towns grew up out of the forests. In 1784, the new colony of New Brunswick was formed. As the years passed, the Loyalists thrived in their new homes.

One group of settlers, however, did not fare so well. For many of Nova Scotia's 3500 Black Loyalists, the new country was a bitter disappointment. Most were denied the support they had been promised, and some received no land at all. Many Black Loyalists left Nova Scotia to seek better lives in other British colonies.

Although the Loyalists soon became the largest group of Atlantic settlers, they were by no means the only group. Long-established settlements of Indians and Acadians carried on much as they had done before. In Newfoundland, fishing settlements were growing as British fishermen decided to live in the colony year-round.

"The Landing of the Loyalists." The first Loyalists sought refuge in the Maritimes. They landed at the mouth of the St. John River in May 1783.

JOSEPH DES BARRES   1722–1824

Mapmaker of the Atlantic

Joseph Des Barres was a Protestant Frenchman from England. He first came to North America at the start of the Seven Years War. He became *General Wolfe*'s aide-de-camp at Quebec.

Des Barres was reporting to Wolfe when the general received his fatal wound. Struck down by French bullets, Wolfe died in the arms of a Frenchman.

2 After the American Revolution, Des Barres helped to settle Loyalist refugees in British North America. In 1784, he became the first lieutenant-governor of Cape Breton Island.

1 When the war ended in 1763, Des Barres went to live in the Maritimes. He spent the next ten years charting the coast of Nova Scotia. In 1777, he produced an excellent sailors' guide to the North Atlantic Coast. This was called "The Atlantic Neptune."

3 Des Barres founded the town of Sydney and opened the valuable coal fields there. When he was 82, he became lieutenant-governor of Prince Edward Island. He retired at 90, but could still dance a jig on a table when he was 100!

Ambassador of the Inuit

Mikak was a Labrador Inuk, the daughter of an Inuit chief. Her people had suffered at the hands of Europeans and wanted to drive the invaders away. In 1767, Mikak's band raided a British fishing station. Her husband was killed, and she and her young son were taken prisoner.

Here is Mikak's story, as her son, Tootac, might have told it to his children:

"The soldiers brought us to Chateau Bay and kept us there for the winter. It was dark and lonely in our blockhouse prison. My mother played games with me and told me stories, but I could see that her heart was heavy. She kept busy though, taking care of me and helping the other Inuit prisoners.

"Before long, the British soldiers saw that my mother was wise and respected by our people. One of their leaders, Francis Lucas, tried to make friends with her. Over the months, he taught my mother English. By summer, she could speak English well and even taught some to me.

"In the fall, Lucas asked my mother if she would like to visit England. My mother agreed to go, so long as she could bring me.

"We sailed with Lucas far across the open sea. I did not like the boat much. Sometimes the water towered over us like a cliff. My mother told me I must be strong. We were Labrador Inuit, she said. All our lives we bravely faced great dangers.

"The English people admired my mother, and treated her with great respect. To them, she was

John Russell painted this portrait of Mikak and her son Tootac during their stay in England.

'Mikak, the Eskimo princess.' Their most important people came to see her, and the king pinned a medal on her dress. The king's mother, Princess Augusta, gave her a fine gown trimmed with gold lace. Today, my own wife wears it.

"In London, my mother met a Moravian missionary named Jens Haven. She had known him in Labrador years before and was happy to see him again. He told her he needed land to build a mission among our people. My mother asked her powerful British friends for help, and they agreed.

"Soon I began to long for the white stillness of our land. At last, when summer came, my mother and I sailed home with Lucas. For the first time in two years. we were truly free."

Mikak's story did not end with her return from England. The next summer, Jens Haven arrived to build his Labrador mission. Mikak greeted him, looking proud and majestic in her golden gown. Beside her stood Tuglavina, her new husband, well known for his fiery spirit.

Haven was polite to Mikak, but warned her he would punish her people if they stole from him. Mikak grew angry at this insult. "I am sorry you think so poorly of our people," she said coldly. "But do not the English also steal?"

Mikak forgave Haven and helped him to find a site for his mission. She refused to live at the mission however. She preferred life among her own people, where she could truly be free.

JOHN MARRANT 1755–1791

A Living Sermon

Even as a boy, John Marrant refused to let the world stand in his way. As a freeborn Black in the American South, he grew up struggling against bigotry and injustice. He managed to get an education, although many Blacks were forbidden to read or write. He left school at 11, then studied music for two years.

When Marrant was 13, he went to a Methodist prayer meeting. His heart was stirred by the words of the preacher, and he became a Christian. When his family objected, he left home and disappeared into the forests of South Carolina. Somehow he survived until an Indian hunter found him and took him captive.

For the next two years, Marrant lived as a prisoner of the Cherokee. He learned to live like the Cherokee in the wilderness. When he was 15, he escaped at last.

During the American Revolution, Marrant served as a musician in the Royal Navy. After he was wounded, he went to live in England. In 1785, a letter arrived from his brother in Nova Scotia.

Marrant's brother was one of the thousands of Black Loyalists who had helped Britain in the Revolution. They had been promised new lives in Nova Scotia, but many had found poverty and injustice.

Marrant made up his mind quickly. He would go to Nova Scotia as a missionary and help his people to rise above their troubles. He crossed the Atlantic and preached his first sermon at

Birchtown. For the next four years, he toured the Black settlements of Nova Scotia, spreading his message of strength and perseverance.

As Marrant travelled through the province, he formed his listeners into all-Black chapels so they could keep on meeting. Many White preachers resented Marrant for taking their Black church-goers away from them. The all-Black chapels had a great impact on the lives of the Black Loyalists. They were centres where the people could come together to form their own vibrant culture.

Marrant's fame soon spread far beyond Nova Scotia. He wrote a book based on his life, and it was a huge success. Marrant used his life-story as a sermon to show how far he had come by believing in himself. He wanted to inspire others, especially Blacks, to follow his example and rise above their hardships.

HOW THEY LIVED

It was Christmas morning, and the sun had not yet risen over the little fishing outport of Saint Mary's. Katie Gill wrapped a shawl around her shoulders and slipped out into the deep snow. She picked up some logs from the woodpile and hurried back inside.

Katie was just 15, but she had kept house since her mother's death. She dropped the logs by the big open hearth and knelt down to start a fire. First she checked at the back of the fireplace to make sure the Yule log was still smouldering. It would be bad luck if the log stopped burning before the twelfth day after Christmas.

Soon the black iron kettle was singing in the fireplace. Katie laid plates on the table for Christmas breakfast.

"Oranges!" breathed a small voice. Katie turned to see Molly, standing with Peter on the stairs. Molly raced down and grabbed her orange from the table. Katie laughed at her little sister. This was the only fresh fruit Molly would eat all winter.

By now, the sun was almost up. Father came down the stairs, stretching and yawning. He ruffled Molly's hair and sat down heavily by the hearth. Katie brought him some strong black tea in a tin mug.

Katie crossed the room to the pine chest under the window. She took out a bundle wrapped in cloth, then laid it on the table in front of the others. Molly stood on tiptoe and pulled the bundle open.

"Oohh!" she gasped, grabbing a rag doll by its red wool hair.

Peter unfolded his present, a heavy woollen pullover. In the spring, he would go out fishing for the first time in his father's boat. Then he would need the sweater to keep him warm and dry.

The day passed peacefully and happily. Late in the morning, the Gills heard Mass at Saint Mary's Church on the hill. Then they trudged home through the snow to a fine Christmas dinner of roast wild duck and suet pudding.

After dinner, Father heaved himself from the table with a contented groan. He took his hunting gun from its place above the hearth and walked outside. As the children watched, he raised his gun high in the air and fired. Around the harbour, other fishermen did the same. Christmas visits were about to begin.

Katie cleared the table and hung the kettle over the fire for tea. Then she brought out the rich dark Christmas cake she had baked a month before.

There was a loud knocking and a jangling of bells at the door. "Will ye let the janneys in?" screeched a high-pitched voice. The "janneys" were other people from the village, dressed up in disguise for Christmas visits.

"Come in and welcome," boomed Father, and Peter flung open the door. In stepped three janneys, all in bright costumes. One carried sleigh bells, and another hoisted a fiddle.

"Give us a song!" cried Father, sweeping Molly up on his shoulders. The fiddler struck up a lively tune, and the other janneys started dancing a reel. Father joined in, clapping his large hands to beat the time, with Molly still on his shoulders.

All evening, janneys came and went until Katie could hardly keep her eyes open. She chased Molly and Peter to bed, then stoked the fire so it would burn long into the night.

Katie smiled fondly at her father, asleep and snoring in his hard chair by the hearth. She gave thanks that he was home for Christmas, warm and safe from the sea. Then she turned down the lamp and tiptoed upstairs to bed.

A Loyalist Dreamer

"Ned" Winslow grew up in Massachusetts in a fine mansion by the sea. From its windows, he could look out on Plymouth Rock, where his ancestors had come on the *Mayflower*. Winslow loved the stately British traditions of his colony. He despised the "cursed, venal, worthless rascals" who wanted to end those traditions.

When the American Revolution started, Winslow joined the British army. He went to Halifax, where he became Muster Master General of all Loyalist troops. Winslow loved pomp and ceremony, so he designed his own uniform. He wore a blue coat with plain white buttons, and a scarlet cape with a scarlet lining.

At the war's end, over 6000 Loyalist troops and their families were left homeless. Winslow agreed to find lands for them in Nova Scotia. He could sympathize with his troops, for he too had lost his home. The war had thrown his entire family into poverty and exile.

In the summer of 1783, Winslow landed at the mouth of the Saint John River. He found thousands of Loyalists "crowded into one spot without covering, and totally ignorant of where they are eventually to settle." He was appalled by their plight, especially when his old troops arrived with their hungry families. He started directing surveys and handing out grants of lands.

Winslow could see beyond the hardships of the Loyalists to a bright future in the new country. He saw the wilderness as a challenge, a chance to build a brand new society. Restless to begin, he explored almost 200 kilometres of the Saint John River. He returned "delighted beyond expression."

Winslow began to dream of forming a separate Loyalist colony to the north of the Bay of

Fundy. Life in this province would be calm and orderly, a tribute to British traditions. The people would be cultured and polite, and they would build stately, beautiful homes. "By God!" declared Winslow. "We will be the envy of the American states."

Winslow's vision soon caught fire among the Loyalists. They formed a "partition movement" to push the plan through. In June 1784, the Loyalist province of New Brunswick was born.

The new Loyalist colony turned out to be a bit more democratic than Winslow had counted on. "Our gentlemen have all become potato farmers," he grumbled. "And our shoemakers are preparing to legislate."

HENRY ALLINE   1748–1784

Preacher of the "New Light"

Eva Scott painted this impression of Alline in 1983.

Henry Alline grew up a strict Puritan in Falmouth, Nova Scotia. In 1775, when he was 27, he became a preacher.

Alline had a vision that told him to spread God's word through Nova Scotia. He started the New Light Movement, which soon became wildly popular. His preaching sparked a religious revival called the "Great Awakening."

1 Alline took his message to Nova Scotia's most remote settlements. He was a fiery speaker and a fine singer. Excited crowds gathered wherever he went.

2 The American Revolution broke out in 1775, the same year Alline had his vision. Alline denounced the Americans as rebels and sinners. His fierce speeches stopped many Nova Scotians from joining the Revolution.

3 Alline preached in Nova Scotia for seven years. He also worked with the sick and found time to write more than 500 hymns. He died at the young age of 35, probably from tuberculosis.

In the early 1700s, "Bering the Daring" and others from Russia explored the icebound northern stretches of North America's west coast. They laid claim to the area now known as Alaska. In the mid-1700s, Spanish seamen explored the coast further south. Spain had already claimed this land as part of its vast empire.

Then, in 1778, *Captain James Cook* landed at Nootka Sound on present-day Vancouver Island. He spent nearly a month there, repairing his ships and getting to know the Moachat Indians. Cook claimed the new land for Britain.

Within ten years of Cook's landing, British otter-fur traders reached Nootka Sound. They began to buy furs from the Indians and their powerful chief, *Muquinna*. In 1789, Spanish warships arrived to contest Britain's claim to the Coast. However, when Britain threatened to declare war, Spain backed down.

The British sent *George Vancouver* to Nootka Sound to make sure their claim held. With Muquinna's help, Vancouver made peace with the Spanish captain, *Juan Bodega y Quadra*. The two became friends, and Vancouver named the island "Vancouver's and Quadra's Island."

By the late 1700s, Britain had a much clearer picture of its new Pacific lands. Cook and Vancouver spent years exploring and surveying the coastline by ship. Meanwhile, from the other side of the continent, traders pushed toward the Pacific by land.

"Man of Nootka Sound." The artist, John Webber, travelled on one of Cook's ships. Cook always took along artists to sketch the people and places he saw.

Forgotten Adventurers

Esperanza Inlet... Estevan Point... Galiano Island... These romantic place names echo along British Columbia's coast like memories from a distant past. They are Spanish names, and date back to a group of explorers almost forgotten today.

"Don Juan Bodega y Quadra."

Juan de Fuca and Don Juan Perez

In 1494, the Pope boldly divided all the New World between Spain and Portugal. The agreement gave Spain all of North America's Pacific Coast, including the shores of present-day British Columbia.

In 1592, Spain sent a pilot named Juan de Fuca to explore the northern Pacific coast. De Fuca wrote about a strait he found near present-day Vancouver Island. Much later, the narrow water passage south of Vancouver Island was called "Juan de Fuca Strait" in his honour.

For the next 150 years, few sailors ventured north from Mexico along the Pacific coast. Then, in the mid-1700s, the Spanish heard that Russian fur traders were in the North Pacific. The Spanish governor of Mexico grew angry at this challenge to Spain's dominion.

In 1774, Don Juan Perez sailed north from Mexico to secure Spain's North Pacific claims. He ran into storm after storm as he made his way slowly up the fogbound coast.

Despite the hardships of the voyage, Perez managed to sail as far north as the present-day Queen Charlotte Islands. His supplies ran low, however, and he was forced to turn back. He returned to Mexico without ever landing on the Pacific coast. Today, the name "Juan Perez Sound" is the only trace of his visit.

Don Bruno Hecata and Juan Bodega y Quadra

"Spanish Insult to the British Flag." This dramatic engraving shows the Spanish seizing British ships in Nootka Sound. The incident almost started a war between Spain and Britain in Europe.

In 1775, two more ships sailed north up the coast from Mexico. Don Bruno Hecata, the captain of one, reached the west coast of present-day Vancouver Island. No one knows for sure whether he landed.

Juan Bodega y Quadra, captain of the other ship, sailed farther north. When he reached an island near present-day Prince Rupert, he claimed the land for Spain.

Quadra's claim did not last long. In 1778, *James Cook* landed on the Northern Pacific coast and claimed it for Britain. British traders soon followed, much to the anger of Spain. A Spanish fleet captured some British trading ships, but Spain backed down when Britain threatened war.

In 1792, Quadra returned to the North Pacific. This time he went there to turn the coast over to Britain.

Over the years, Spain's claim in the North Pacific faded from memory. All that was left of the Spanish seamen were a few exotic names along the misty coasts they had once explored.

Explorer, Navigator, Map-Maker

Captain James Cook was one of Britain's most famous explorers. He sailed around the world three times and was the first to make the journey from west to east.

Few people know, however, that Cook spent half his career in the waters of present-day Canada. He was the first European to visit Canada on both its Atlantic and Pacific coasts.

2 In 1759, Cook charted the rocks, shoals, and sandbars of the treacherous St. Lawrence River. Using Cook's charts, over 200 British ships sailed safely up the river to capture Quebec.

1 Cook came to North America in the Seven Years War, and took part in the capture of Louisbourg. He worked as a surveyor and learned how to make detailed maps of the coastline.

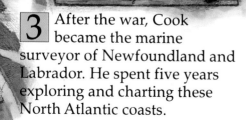

3 After the war, Cook became the marine surveyor of Newfoundland and Labrador. He spent five years exploring and charting these North Atlantic coasts.

4 Between 1768 and 1779, Cook made three great voyages around the world. He explored many lands, especially in the South Pacific. He proved his men could stay healthy with fresh food and clean, dry quarters.

6 Cook always took along painters and wildlife experts to study the places he visited. He learned a great deal about Nootka Sound and the friendly Indians who lived there.

5 In 1778, Cook became the first European to land formally on Canada's west coast. He landed at Nootka Sound, on present-day Vancouver Island.

7 In the next few months, Cook charted almost 5000 kilometres of North Pacific coastline. When cliffs of pack ice blocked his way, he turned south to winter in Hawaii. There he was killed in a clash with angry Polynesians.

Trader and Peacemaker

In March 1778, *Captain James Cook* steered his storm-battered ships into Nootka Sound, on present-day Vancouver Island. Suddenly, from out of the stillness, an Indian canoe appeared, then another. Soon, over 30 canoes surrounded the ships. Cook began to grow alarmed.

In one of the canoes, a handsome chief rose and addressed the captain. With relief, Cook heard the sound of welcome in his voice. Cook never named this chief, but he was almost certainly Muquinna.

Chief Muquinna was the leader of the Moachat people who lived at the mouth of Nootka Sound. He was a striking-looking man, with a strong face and a dignified bearing.

Like other Pacific Coast Indians, Muquinna was an experienced trader. He soon realized that the newcomers from Europe offered a chance for rich profits. His people brought furs to Cook's men and began to bargain.

Cook was not prepared for the sharp business sense of Muquinna and his people. The Moachats knew that Cook's beads and toys were worthless. They insisted on metal they could use, especially brass. Before long, Cook's men had traded away all the metal they owned. They even cut the brass buttons off their uniforms!

Muquinna's people were soon buying furs cheaply from nearby tribes. Then they sold them to Cook's men at a profit. By the time Cook's short visit ended, the Moachats had set up the start of a trading empire.

"Muquinna Entertaining Vancouver." This scene was painted by *Juan Bodega y Quadra*, the Spanish explorer and ambassador. Muquinna helped *Vancouver* and Quadra settle the peace between their countries.

In 1789, a Spanish warship captured the boats of a British trader. Muquinna protested because warfare was bad for his people's trade. However, he soon made peace with the Spanish, partly to protect his people from attack. He told the British he would take their side only if he saw larger British ships.

As time passed, Spain and Britain settled their argument peacefully. In 1792, each country sent an ambassador to Nootka Sound to settle its claim there. *Juan Bodega y Quadra* arrived first for Spain. Then *George Vancouver* arrived to speak for England.

Muquinna was a skilful diplomat and played a key role in the peace talks. Both sides tried to win his favour, but he was careful to remain fair. He was delighted to help restore peace so his people would prosper once more. Under his watchful eye, Vancouver and Quadra soon reached an agreement.

In 1795, Muquinna fell ill with a fever. He died in the autumn and was greatly mourned by his people. Muquinna had guided the Moachats through their first contact with Europeans. He had managed to turn a time of great change to his people's favour.

Mapmaker of the Pacific Coast

George Vancouver was a complex man, with many sides to his nature. He was a harsh commander, yet he devoted great care to the health of his men. He was impatient, and he hurt his career by making powerful enemies. Yet he was also a gracious diplomat, who charmed Indians and Spaniards alike.

Vancouver set out early on his life of high adventure. When he was only 14, he went to sea with *Captain James Cook*. In 1778, he landed with Cook at Nootka Sound, on present-day Vancouver Island. He also took part in Cook's survey of the North Pacific coastline.

In 1790, Vancouver became captain of his own ship, the *Discovery*. He was told to go to Nootka Sound and settle the Spanish claim to the North Pacific coast. While he was there, he could search the Pacific coastline for a water passage from the East.

Vancouver hit on a simple plan for his survey of the coast. He would simply trace every foot of shoreline as far as Alaska!

Vancouver began his survey just north of San Francisco. At first the work seemed easy. However, when he reached present-day British Columbia, he saw how hard it would be. The northern Pacific coastline was a maze of narrow, dangerous inlets.

Vancouver and his men had to leave their ships to enter the inlets in small open boats. Tossed by treacherous winds and tides, and driven by powerful currents, the seamen traced

Until very recently, this painting was thought to be a portrait of Vancouver. Historians now think it is a picture of someone else. No true portrait of Vancouver is known to exist.

each inlet to its head. They took enough food for a week or ten days, but their journeys often proved much longer.

In 1792, Vancouver went to Nootka Sound to meet *Juan Bodega y Quadra*, a representative from Spain. With help from the local chief, *Muquinna*, the two explorers settled their countries' claims.

"Captain George Vancouver, at English Bay, near Entrance to Burrard Inlet —Pacific Coast."

Vancouver and Quadra liked each other and quickly became warm friends. Vancouver had just learned that Nootka Sound was part of a large island. He named this "Vancouver's and Quadra's Island" to honour his new friend. Much later, it became Vancouver Island.

Vancouver returned to his survey and pushed further up the coast. As he traced the shoreline, he kept careful notes of scenery and landmarks. He studied the animal and plant life, and gave English names to over 200 places.

In 1794, Vancouver finally completed his survey. It had taken four and a half years and was the longest survey in history. By the time he returned home, Vancouver had sailed over 100 000 kilometres by ship. He and his men had covered another 16 000 kilometres in small open boats.

Weary and ill after his long voyage, Vancouver was glad to reach England. Instead of praise and recognition, however, he found only criticism. His outbursts of temper had offended some of his officers, and they had complained in high places. Sick and disappointed, he retreated to the country to write the story of his travels.

Vancouver died before he could finish his book, but his brother completed it for him. The work, in six large volumes, was soon praised as a masterpiece of surveying. Vancouver's charts gave the world a clear picture of the North Pacific Coast. Sailors would rely on his fine maps for over a hundred years.

THE GREAT NORTHWEST

After the Seven Years War, only a few French fur traders stayed in the West. In their place came English-speaking adventurers with a taste for independence. The Hudson's Bay Company called these traders the "pedlars from Quebec."

The pedlars employed French Canadian voyageurs and took over the old French trade routes. As the years passed, some of the pedlars began to form groups. In 1779, they came together to form the great North West Company.

"Je suis un homme du nord!" This was the cry of the North West Company traders, the brave Nor'Westers. These men ranged freely through the vast Canadian Northwest, searching for furs and adventure. They scorned the less spirited traders who worked for the older Hudson's Bay Company.

Unlike Hudson's Bay traders, the Nor'Westers had no direct waterway into the fur lands of the West. They had to canoe up the St. Lawrence water route, then carry their goods on long overland portages. Their route was slow, hard, and costly.

To keep up with their rivals, the Nor'Westers had to explore new lands in search of furs. They journeyed far into the interior to intercept Indians who were bringing pelts to the Hudson's Bay posts. They searched for a way through the Rocky Mountains so they could ship their furs to Britain from the Pacific coast. Many had Indian wives, who helped expand their trade.

The adventurous Nor'Westers soon became the leaders of western exploration. To compete with their rivals, they opened up the vast new lands of the Canadian Northwest.

"Mackenzie Crossing the Rockies" by Arthur Heming.

The Lawless Pedlar

When Peter Pond was barely 16, he defied his parents and joined the British Army. After the Seven Years War, he returned home to Milford, Connecticut and tried to settle down. The western wilderness soon called him, however, and he left his wife and children to join the fur trade.

Pond was a restless and hot-tempered man. When trading in the Detroit region, he quarrelled with another trader. The two men fought a duel, and Pond won.

In 1775, Pond's search for better furs brought him to the Canadian Northwest. He explored much of this rich new land and opened it up to the fur trade. He joined the group of traders who would soon form the North West Company.

In 1781, Pond quarrelled with Jean-Etienne Waddens, a competing trader at Lac la Ronge. No one knows whether Pond or his clerk shot Waddens. When Waddens' widow charged Pond with murder, she was told that Lac la Ronge was outside the reach of Quebec law.

Although Pond had little education, he had a very inquiring mind. He asked the Indians many questions about lands west of Lake Athabasca. Using their answers, he drew some maps that were surprisingly close to the truth. Pond shared many of his ideas with the great explorer, *Alexander Mackenzie*.

In 1787, Pond was trading at his post on Lake Athabasca. A rival trader, John Ross, accused him of forcing Indians to trade with him. A fight broke out, and Ross was killed. Although Pond was not there himself, many believed he ordered the shooting. His fellow traders drove him out of the North West Company.

Pond spent his last years in poverty and died a forgotten man. Even his journal was considered worthless—its last pages were used to start a kitchen fire.

A Bold Adventurer

As a boy in England, Samuel Hearne dreamed of a life at sea. He joined the Royal Navy when he was only 11 and served in the Seven Years War. When he was 20, he joined the Hudson's Bay Company as a sailor. He was sent to Fort Prince of Wales, at the mouth of the Churchill River.

2 Hearne was soon busy exploring the lands west of the bay. He often ran out of food and had to eat old leather and charred bones. Later he learned survival from the Indians of the area, adopting their customs and eating their food.

1 Hearne's greatest wish was to captain his own ship. After four years of service, he thought he was ready for promotion. Instead, the Company sent him to explore the interior by land.

3 Hearne made two trips in search of a river the Indians said was rich in copper. In December 1770, he set out again with his friend *Chief Matonabbee*. The chief took along Indian women because they could carry more than men.

4 After seven months, Hearne reached the Coppermine River. He followed it to the Arctic Ocean and claimed the coast for the Hudson's Bay Company. A hundred years would pass before Europeans returned to this barren shore.

5 The Hudson's Bay Company began to lose business to the independent "pedlars" who controlled the interior. In 1774, Hearne was sent to find a place for the Company's first inland trading post. His search took him farther west than traders had ever been.

6 Hearne chose a site near the Saskatchewan River, where the lands of three Indian tribes met. Cumberland House was the first of the Company's many inland posts.

7 In his two epic journeys, Samuel Hearne travelled many thousands of kilometres on foot through treacherous lands. He described his exciting adventures in a journal, which can still be read today.

MATONABBEE c. 1737–1782

Ambassador and Explorer

From his birth, Matonabbee's life was divided between two separate worlds. He was born to Indian parents at Fort Prince of Wales on Hudson Bay. The traders at the fort taught Matonabbee the business of the fur trade. His Chipewyan people taught him how to survive in the harsh northern lands.

Intelligent and generous, swift and strong, Matonabbee soon proved invaluable to the Hudson's Bay Company. In his early twenties, he was sent to make peace between the Chipewyans and Cree near Lake Athabasca. He risked his life by going among the Cree as an ambassador. He earned the respect of his enemy and soon brought an end to the conflict.

Through the next years, Matonabbee became very active in the fur trade. He became more successful by far than any Indian trader before him. He ventured far inland to open up trade with the Yellowknife Indians and the Dogribs.

By the late 1760s, Matonabbee had made at least one trip to the fabled Coppermine River. When he showed his rough maps to the Hudson's Bay traders, they decided to send an English explorer there. They chose *Samuel Hearne*, a young seaman with no experience on land.

time they returned from the Arctic Ocean, they had covered over 5000 kilometres.

For the rest of his life, Matonabbee continued to make long successful trading journeys. The traders at Fort Prince of Wales admired him greatly. Whenever he arrived there, they honoured him with feasts, dances, and gifts.

Matonabbee always lived according to his own strict code of honour. He was fiercely loyal to his friends and thought of their joys and sorrows as his own. In 1776, Samuel Hearne became the governor of Fort Prince of Wales. Then, in 1782, Hearne surrendered the fort to a large group of French attackers.

In Matonabbee's fierce code of honour, any surrender was an act of cowardice. Because he thought of Hearne as a brother, he accepted Hearne's shame as his own. Matonabbee took his own life, because he could not stand the disgrace.

In the autumn of 1770, Matonabbee came upon Hearne starving in the wilderness. Hearne had been deserted by his guides and was completely lost. Matonabbee found him food and warm clothes, then took him back to Fort Prince of Wales. During the grinding two-month trek, the two men became friends for life.

Matonabbee offered to guide Hearne on his journey to find the river. For the next year and a half, Matonabbee led the explorer through marshland and drifting snow, over rocks and glacial ice. He found them food and shelter, and he taught Hearne how to live in the wilds. By the

First Overland to the Pacific

Alexander Mackenzie was a restless, high-spirited boy, who longed for great adventure. When he was 15, he left school in Montreal to become a fur trader. He joined the North West Company in 1787, and took over its Athabasca post the next year.

Mackenzie was eager to find an overland route to the Pacific Ocean. In June 1789, he set out to explore the lands west of Lake Athabasca.

3 Mackenzie started at once to plan a second voyage. This time he wanted to be better prepared. He visited London to buy proper equipment.

1 Battered by storms and tormented by mosquitoes, Mackenzie made slow progress. After he crossed Great Slave Lake, he reached a mighty river flowing westward. Soon he was travelling 125 kilometres a day!

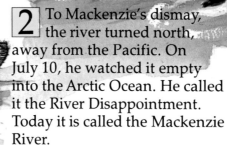

2 To Mackenzie's dismay, the river turned north, away from the Pacific. On July 10, he watched it empty into the Arctic Ocean. He called it the River Disappointment. Today it is called the Mackenzie River.

4 Mackenzie headed west again, this time along the Peace River. As he and his men climbed up the Rockies, they often had to portage over rugged mountain terrain.

6 Weighed down by heavy loads, the party travelled on foot for two weeks. In late July, after a journey of almost 2000 kilometres, Mackenzie sighted the Pacific. He became the first non-Native to reach Canada's west coast by land.

7 Mackenzie had added a vast tract of land to the map of North America. However, the North West Company had little use for his route. Many years would pass before its importance would be understood.

5 After crossing the Great Divide, the explorers came to a wild river, later named the *Fraser*. Mackenzie asked advice from some nearby Indians. They told him the best way to the ocean was overland.

Alex Mackenzie from Canada by land 22^d

Interpreter and Guide

No one knows English Chief's real name. He was a Chipewyan chief who had gone with *Matonabbee* and *Samuel Hearne* to the Coppermine River. In 1789, he set out with *Alexander Mackenzie* to find a river that flowed from Great Slave Lake. Mackenzie hoped to follow the river to the Pacific.

English Chief helped Mackenzie in many ways. He hunted game and shared his vast knowledge of the land. He knew many Indian dialects and acted as Mackenzie's interpreter.

Mackenzie was not an easy man to work for. He drove people hard and expected them to endure great dangers and hardships. Mackenzie travelled from four in the morning until after seven at night. He moved at top speed, sometimes covering 150 kilometres in a day!

English Chief always kept up with Mackenzie's killing pace. He put up with swarms of insects, long portages, and scarce game. At last he stood with Mackenzie at the mouth of the great river. However, English Chief could see that it emptied into the Arctic Ocean, not the Pacific!

As English Chief and Mackenzie were leaving the Arctic, they heard about a river far west across the mountains. Mackenzie wanted to follow this new river to the Pacific. He made plans to cross the mountains right away!

English Chief knew that a journey across the mountains so late in the year would be suicide. He began to discourage the Indians they met from talking about the western river. When Mackenzie grew angry, English Chief refused to go with him any further.

Mackenzie knew how much he needed English Chief's help to get home from the Arctic. He gave in and promised not to seek the western river. English Chief agreed to take Mackenzie safely back to his fort.

That night, English Chief and Mackenzie ate and drank together. Soon, they were better friends than ever.

Chapter Five

DANGER ON ALL SIDES
1812 - 1850

THE WAR OF 1812

In June 1812, the United States declared war on Britain and its colonies. The Americans had been angry for a long time. Britain had forbidden America to trade with its enemy, Napoleon of France. British officers had stopped American ships at gunpoint to search for British deserters. American settlers believed that the British were helping the western Indians to fight for their lands.

Across British North America, people rallied to the defence of their land. Canadian settlers took up muskets and left their crops to wither in the fields. Brave Maritime sailors manned privateers, ships sent out to plunder American vessels. The war claimed many British, Canadian, and Indian lives.

For three long years, the bitter struggle raged along the American border. In 1814, the war at last drew to a close. Britain had almost defeated Napoleon and could send more ships to North America. The Americans realized they would never conquer the colonies, and both sides were tired of fighting. On Christmas Eve, the war came to an end.

The colonies did not gain any land from the war, but they did gain a new sense of national identity. For perhaps the first time, settlers from Upper Canada, Lower Canada, and the Maritimes had come together for a single cause. They had begun to see themselves as one people.

"The American Victory at Lake Erie" by James Webster. The War of 1812 was not fought only on land. Here, American and British ships are fighting for control of the Great Lakes.

CALEB SEELY   1787–1869

A Gallant Privateersman

In the War of 1812, the British navy had help from the Atlantic privateersmen. These bold seamen ranged the Atlantic coast, capturing and plundering enemy ships. To some, they were rogues and scoundrels, "legal pirates" on the high seas. To others, they were gallant heroes, waging a brave sea war against the Americans.

Caleb Seely was a young privateersman from Saint John, New Brunswick. Tall and handsome, he was still a boy when he first went to sea. In 1813, when he was 26, he took command of the *Star*, a privateer schooner. He soon captured three American ships and took his share of the booty.

As captain of a privateer, Seely had to follow strict rules, or he could be hanged for piracy. He carried a licence signed by the British governor. He could only attack enemy vessels, or those trading with the enemy. He had to take captured ships to Halifax, where a naval court ruled on his actions.

In late 1813, Seely took command of a privateer called the *Liverpool Packet*. The *Packet* was already a legend on the Atlantic coast. Swift and sleek, it had often pursued ships right into American harbours. Its last captain, Joseph Barss, had captured 30 enemy ships in only 9 months.

Under Caleb Seely, the *Liverpool Packet* continued its legendary forays. For almost a year, Seely raided ships up and down the New England coast. Once, in four days, he captured booty worth more than $100 000. Seely was a gallant captain, and he treated his prisoners well.

After the war, Seely settled down to a more peaceful life. He moved to England and built up a shipping business. He outlived three wives and died quietly at the age of 81.

Saviour of Upper Canada

Isaac Brock was every inch a hero. Tall, broad-shouldered, and muscular, he towered over the people around him. He was a brilliant officer, a superb horseman, and an excellent swimmer and boxer. He enjoyed good food and lively company, and he was known as a spirited dancer.

Brock joined the army as a boy of 15, and soon made a name for himself. He was only 28 when he took charge of his own regiment. When Brock took command, the 49th Regiment was one of the worst in the army. Brock won his men's respect and soon turned them into a crack outfit.

Brock became a general in 1811 and was placed in charge of Upper Canada. Right away, he began to prepare for war with the United States.

When war broke out in 1812, Brock acted quickly to rally support. "Most of the people have lost all confidence," he wrote. "I however speak loud and look big." He ordered a bold surprise attack on the American fort at Michilimackinac. His victory stirred the hearts of the Canadian people.

Brock soon proved himself a brilliant and daring leader in war. His soldiers loved him and were prepared to follow him anywhere.

Brock wanted the western Indians to join the Canadian side. He needed their skill and courage to make up for his shortage of men. Soon after the war began, he met with their great leader, the Shawnee chief *Tecumseh*.

The lithe, deerskin-clad Indian took an instant liking to the towering British general. "This is a *man*!" reported Tecumseh to his warriors.

A few days later, Brock and Tecumseh attacked a larger American force at Detroit. Through a brilliant trick, they convinced the

"Death of Brock at Queenston Heights." Today a huge statue of Brock marks the place where he was killed.

Americans that they were hopelessly outnumbered. The American general surrendered without firing a shot. The stunning victory showed Canadians they could win the war.

On a blustery October morning, Brock was wakened before dawn by the sound of cannons in the distance. A large American force had crossed the Niagara River at Queenston, 11 kilometres away. Within minutes, Brock was galloping toward the sounds of battle on his grey charger, Alfred. When his men saw him coming, they cheered.

Brock was soon in the thick of the fighting. When he saw the Americans had taken Queenston Heights, he prepared a direct attack.

"Follow me!" he shouted as he stormed up the hill at the head of 200 men.

In his crimson uniform and plumed hat, Brock's huge figure made an easy target. A bullet struck his wrist, but he went on. Then an American rifleman stepped from behind some trees. He aimed carefully, fired once, and Isaac Brock fell dead.

Brock's soldiers were stunned, but they soon rallied. Quickly they spread the word: "Revenge the General!" That day, the Battle of Queenston Heights ended with a Canadian victory.

TECUMSEH 1768–1813

Leader of the Western Tribes

Tecumseh grew up in the Ohio lands south of the Great Lakes. When he was just a small boy, his father was killed by American settlers. Tecumseh's older brother, Cheeseekau, trained him as a warrior and taught him the Shawnee code of honour.

These were hard years for Tecumseh's people. The Shawnee had always roamed freely through the land south of the Great Lakes. Now American settlers were pushing into those lands and driving the western Indians away.

Tecumseh was only 15 when he fought his first battle with the Americans. Over the next years, he fought many more battles as his people were forced from their homes.

Like *Pontiac* before him, Tecumseh began to dream of uniting the western tribes. Then they could take back their lands south of the Great Lakes and form an independent Indian state.

Tecumseh travelled as far south as Florida spreading his dream among the western tribes. With the help of his brother, he set up a large village at Tippecanoe, south of Lake Michigan. Then, while he was away, the Americans attacked the village and burned it to the ground. Tecumseh decided the time had come for war.

When the War of 1812 broke out, Tecumseh led 600 warriors into Upper Canada to join the Canadians and British. Tecumseh took an instant liking to the British general, *Isaac Brock*.

To keep the Americans out of Upper Canada, Brock and Tecumseh first had to capture Fort Detroit. They knew they were badly outnumbered by the Americans in the fort. Together, the two leaders came up with a daring plan.

On the day of the battle, Tecumseh led his 600 warriors in single file across a clearing in front of the fort. Then he doubled back into the forests and led them around twice more! The confused Americans thought they saw thousands of fierce warriors preparing to attack. They surrendered without firing a shot.

In late 1812, General Brock was killed. The new leader, Colonel Procter, was weak and untrustworthy. Without consulting Tecumseh, he decided to retreat from Detroit.

"The Battle of the Thames." Tecumseh was wearing a British officer's sash when he was killed. *Isaac Brock* had given him the sash as a token of esteem.

Tecumseh begged Procter for enough arms to carry on the fight himself. When Procter refused, Tecumseh and his warriors were forced to join the retreat. Finally, north of Lake Erie, Tecumseh shamed Procter into turning and taking a stand.

The Battle of the Thames was to be Tecumseh's last. The British troops broke line and fled, leaving 600 Indians to face 3000 Americans. Tecumseh fought bravely, but the odds against him were too great. He died a hero's death, in the midst of flaming battle.

It was not long before Tecumseh's dream died with him. Without their great leader to bring them together, the western tribes broke their alliance. Britain soon forgot its Indian general and did not help his people regain their lands.

LAURA SECORD   1775–1868

Heroine of Beaver Dams

Laura Secord was typical of many settlers in Upper Canada during the early 1800s. She had left the United States with her Loyalist family after the American Revolution. She had married in 1797 and settled down in Queenston. When the War of 1812 broke out, she found herself in the heart of the battle zone.

2 Laura rushed straight to the battlefield. After a frantic search, she found her injured husband and took him home. James was sick for many months, but Laura's bravery probably saved his life.

1 James Secord was a militia sergeant in the Battle of Queenston Heights. He was wounded on the same day that *General Brock* was killed. Laura was horrified when she heard that her husband was hurt.

3 The next June, the Secords were forced to let enemy soldiers live in their house. One night, Laura overheard the Americans planning to attack the British and Canadian troops at Beaver Dams.

4 Laura decided she must warn the British commander, Lieutenant Colonel James FitzGibbon. She slipped out of the house before dawn the next day to begin a 30-kilometre trek through rough country.

6 Laura told the astonished FitzGibbon about the planned attack on his troops. He immediately sent a force of Indians to wait for the enemy. Two days later, the Indians ambushed and defeated the American attackers.

5 By sunset, Laura was exhausted from her rugged journey. Suddenly a group of Indians blocked her path. The Indian chief was an ally of the British. When Laura told him her story, he agreed to take her to FitzGibbon's house.

7 Laura's heroism was soon forgotten and she lived in poverty for many years. Then, in 1860, the Prince of Wales visited Canada and heard Laura's story. He later sent her a reward of £100—nearly 50 years after her brave walk!

Defender of Montreal

No wolf or tiger
Could be so fierce!
Under the open sky
He has no equal!

So sang the Voltigeur soldiers about their brave leader, Colonel Charles-Michel de Salaberry. The colonel was a French Canadian aristocrat, who lived by a strict code of honour. He was also a man of action, who carried a scar across his forehead from a duel. Short and muscular, he was fearless in battle. His superior called him "my dear marquis of cannon powder."

De Salaberry had led a soldier's life since he was 15. He had fought against Napoleon's armies in Europe and the West Indies. Soon after he returned to Canada, war broke out with America.

De Salaberry took charge of the Chateauguay frontier, south of Montreal. He recruited a force of French Canadians, the famous Voltigeurs. The Voltigeurs were voyageurs, lumbermen, and young men from the cities. De Salaberry drilled them relentlessly until they were top soldiers, at home in the woods or on the battlefield.

In 1813, the Americans decided to attack Montreal and gain control of the St. Lawrence River. In late October, over 4000 American soldiers crossed the Canadian border. All that stood between them and Montreal were Colonel de Salaberry and a few hundred men.

Despite the odds against him, de Salaberry did not hesitate. He prepared a battleground at a bend in the Chateauguay River, using some

ravines as trenches. He arranged his men to make it seem as if there were more of them. Then he settled back to await the enemy.

The Americans soon saw it would be harder to beat de Salaberry than they had thought. One group of Americans plunged into the forest to try to surround the Canadians. In the dark, rainy night, the troops lost their way. The next morning, some of them found themselves beside, not behind, de Salaberry's men. De Salaberry opened fire, and they scattered.

The remaining Americans decided to attack head-on. To trick them, de Salaberry sent buglers into the woods. He ordered them to trumpet in all directions so the Americans would think they were outnumbered. He also sent Indian troops into the woods to fool the enemy with their battle cries.

"The Battle of Chateauguay." De Salaberry directed his troops as if they were actors in a play. By creating the illusion of a strong army, he saved Montreal from invasion.

De Salaberry ordered some of his men to appear once in their red jackets, then again with their white linings turned inside out. That way, the Americans counted them twice!

De Salaberry's plan worked. In the brief battle that followed, he urged his men on boldly. "Defy, defy!" he cried. "If you do not dare, you are not men!" The Americans believed they were facing at least 5000 soldiers. Rather than lose more lives, the Americans broke column and withdrew.

De Salaberry's deed soon became a legend across the land. Outnumbered by more than four to one, he had saved Montreal from attack!

THE FUR TRADE WARS

Over the years, the North West Company and Hudson's Bay Company had become bitter rivals for the fur trade. Hudson's Bay traders accused the Nor'Westers of trespassing on their lands. They denied the Nor'Westers access to Hudson Bay, forcing them to ship furs by a much harder route.

In 1811, Lord Selkirk of the Hudson's Bay Company invited homeless Scottish farmers to settle on the banks of the Red River. The first Selkirk settlers arrived in 1812, after a hard journey overland from Hudson Bay.

The Nor'Westers believed that the Hudson's Bay Company was sending the settlers to destroy them. The Nor'Westers needed the Red River to send their furs to Montreal. They also needed buffalo meat from the Red River Métis.

The Métis were part European and part Indian, with their own unique way of life. They made their living by hunting buffalo in the Red River lands. Then they made the meat into pemmican and sold it to the fur traders as food.

In their first years, the Selkirk settlers came close to starving. Their governor, Miles Macdonell, forbade the Métis and Nor'Westers to take pemmican away from the Red River area.

The Métis and the Nor'Westers depended on the pemmican trade for their survival. They decided to drive the settlers away. Over the next years, they fought many battles with the settlers and Hudson's Bay traders.

The "fur trade wars" were finally settled in 1821. The Hudson's Bay Company absorbed the North West Company and became a vast fur-trading empire. The days of the great Nor'Westers were over.

"Half Breeds Running Buffalo" by *Paul Kane*. The Métis hunted buffalo for their living. They grew angry when the Scottish settlers made claim to the buffalo in the Red River Valley.

SIMON FRASER   1776–1862

White Water Explorer

Simon Fraser was only 16 when he joined the North West Company. In 1805, he built Trout Lake Post, the first permanent European settlement west of the Canadian Rockies.

In 1808, Fraser set out to survey the Columbia River. He was determined to find a trade route to the Pacific.

2 When travel by water became impossible, Fraser refused to turn back. He greatly admired the skill of his Indian guides: "They went on boldly with heavy loads in places where we were obliged to hand our guns from one to another."

1 Fraser soon found that the river was wild and treacherous. He and his men had to carry their canoes through rough country to avoid shoals and waterfalls. When high, steep banks stopped them from landing, they were forced to shoot the rapids.

3 Fraser reached the mouth of the river at last, only to find it was not the Columbia at all. He had explored another unknown river, far to the Columbia's north. Fittingly, it was later named the Fraser River.

DAVID THOMPSON   1770–1857

Wizard of the Wilderness

David Thompson spent his first years in an English school for poor orphans. It was a cold, dreary life for a small boy. To escape from it, he began to read books about travel and sea-faring. He dreamed of a life of adventure in faraway places.

When Thompson was 14, his wish began to come true. The Hudson's Bay Company wanted boys to work at its trading posts in Canada. Because of the books he had read, Thompson was picked. The Company paid the school about $15 for him.

At first, Thompson worked as a clerk for the company, then as a trader. As he grew older, he learned how to survey the land and make maps. Despite very poor eyesight, Thompson had a special talent for finding his way in the wilderness. Even the Indians were impressed, and some called him a wizard.

Thompson longed to set off and explore new lands. As time passed, however, he could see that the Hudson's Bay Company wanted traders, not explorers. One winter, he was trading at Reindeer Lake when he met *Simon Fraser*, of the North West Company. "Join the Nor'Westers," said Fraser. "You can explore all you want with us!"

Thompson took Fraser's advice. Soon he was ranging far and wide, surveying unknown western lands. He travelled thousands of kilometres by foot, canoe, horseback, and snowshoe. On one of his journeys, he stopped just long enough to marry. His bride was Charlotte Small, a spirited Métis girl.

The Nor'Westers had long dreamed of finding a trade route through the Rockies. They knew that a great river called the Columbia emptied into the Pacific. Perhaps its waters could be followed through the mountains.

In 1806, Thompson set out to find and explore the Columbia River. Charlotte went with him, along with their two small children. Together they followed the Saskatchewan River high into the mountains. They struggled up many steep and treacherous mountain trails. They picked their way through glacial ice that no European had ever seen.

At last, Thompson and Charlotte stood atop the Great Divide, a pass through the Rockies. There they found a tiny stream flowing to the west. They followed the stream, and soon they were racing down the mighty Columbia River.

In 1812, Thompson and Charlotte decided to leave the far Northwest. They went to Lower Canada, where Thompson began a huge map of all the lands he had surveyed. This map gave the first clear picture of the vast area between Lake Superior and the Pacific coast. It was hung at Fort William, then headquarters of the North West Company. It almost covered the entire end wall of the Great Mess Hall.

Like many other Nor'Westers, Thompson was quickly forgotten by the world. Many years after his death, his map was rediscovered and hailed as a masterpiece. Thompson was called North America's greatest land geographer.

MARIE-ANNE GABOURY   1780–1875

First Non-Native Woman in the West

When she was 25, Marie-Anne Gaboury married Jean-Baptiste Lagimodière. Jean-Baptiste was a handsome young buffalo hunter, who was in Lower Canada to see his family. He told Marie-Anne how much he missed his life in the great Northwest.

When Jean-Baptiste said he was going back to the Northwest, Marie-Anne decided to go with him.

2 On January 6, 1807, the first non-Native child in the West was born. Because it was the feast of the Three Kings, the little girl was called Reine.

1 The young couple followed the arduous fur-trade route thousands of kilometres north and west. Marie-Anne always faced her share of the hard work and danger.

3 Marie-Anne's new life was filled with danger and adventure. Once her horse ran out of control, straight into a herd of buffalo. Marie-Anne clung on to its mane and prayed. She barely escaped alive.

4 In 1812, other non-Native women came west to join Lord Selkirk's Red River settlement. Marie-Anne and Jean-Baptiste decided to build a home near the colony.

6 While Jean-Baptiste was away, the Nor'Westers attacked the colony. Marie-Anne escaped with her children across the Red River to the camp of *Chief Peguis*. She was so frightened that she fainted in Chief Peguis' canoe!

5 When the North West Company threatened the Red River colony, the settlers asked Jean-Baptiste to take a message to Lord Selkirk. Jean-Baptiste raced over 3000 kilometres by snowshoe and canoe to Montreal.

7 Marie-Anne lived until she was 95 and saw many changes come to her beloved West. She saw her grandson, Louis Riel, grow into one of the land's great leaders.

CATHERINE MCPHERSON   c. 1789–1876

Selkirk Settler

Catherine McPherson had lost everything. The Duchess of Sutherland had burnt down her cottage to clear land for sheep-farming. All over Scotland, other landowners were doing the same thing.

Catherine had heard that Lord Selkirk was starting a colony in the western lands of Canada. In 1813, she set sail from Scotland with more than 90 other settlers. Here is how she might have described the long, hard journey to Red River.

"My heart was light as we bid farewell to the hills and glens of Scotland. I did not guess how many trials we would have to endure.

"After a few days at sea, typhus broke out on our ship. Soon the ship's hold echoed with the groans of the sick and dying. The ship's doctor showed me how to nurse the ill. I bathed their faces with cool water and made warm broths for them to drink.

"The ship's captain could not wait to get rid of his sick passengers. He was supposed to take us to York Factory. Instead, he left us at Fort Churchill, 250 kilometres away.

"We were too weak and sick to walk, so spent the winter where we were. We cut down trees and built ourselves log houses. For weeks we toiled from dawn till dark, cold, hungry, and dizzy with weariness. When we finished, the icy wind still whistled through gaps in the walls.

"The snow was still deep on the ground when we set off on the long trek to York Factory. We walked slowly on our snowshoes, singing brave Scottish songs to the music of Robbie Gunn's bagpipes.

"Some of the men went ahead, dragging their sleds to make a path. I stayed at the rear to help those who fell behind. Many suffered from leg cramps and snow blindness, and I did what I could to nurse them.

"For long cruel days, we stumbled over snow banks and shielded our eyes against the glare. Slowly, our legs grew used to the snowshoes. I walked at the side of Alexander Sutherland, a handsome young man who had been a soldier.

"At York Factory, we had to stop and wait for the Hayes River to thaw. Then we began the journey of 1000 kilometres by water to Red River.

At first, river travel seemed almost restful. Then the land changed, the banks towered above us, and the water flowed fast over sharp rocks.

"Again and again, we unloaded our boats and carried our supplies around rapids and waterfalls. Black flies and mosquitoes tormented us night and day. Then on June 21, after almost a year, we reached Red River at last."

Catherine married Alexander and began to clear land for her home. Soon she would face many more hardships. She would see her house burned, her crops destroyed, and her friends killed in the fur trade war. She would suffer through floods, droughts, plagues of grasshoppers, and epidemics of smallpox. Many settlers would leave, but Catherine and Alexander would stay at Red River to struggle and endure.

Warden of the Plains

Cuthbert Grant was worried. The Hudson's Bay Company was sending Scottish settlers to Red River. For over 100 years, Grant's Métis ancestors had hunted buffalo in the Red River lands. Grant was only 18, but already he was a leader among his people.

The Métis were part Indian and part European. The French called them the *bois-brûlés*, or "burnt-wood people," because of their dark skin. They called themselves the "New Nation," the lords of the prairie.

Grant had good reason to worry about the arrival of the Selkirk settlers. The Métis made their living by hunting the buffalo in the Red River lands. They dried the meat and sold it as pemmican to the fur traders. If settlers began to build farms in the buffalo lands, the Métis way of life might vanish forever.

Grant's fears soon began to come true. The Selkirk settlers began to suffer from lack of food. Their leader, Miles Macdonell, forbade anyone to take pemmican away from the area. Grant was furious. The Métis needed to sell pemmican to make a living.

Macdonell backed down, but then he gave an order that made the Métis even angrier. He said they could not hunt buffalo in the rich lands near the settlement. For Grant, this was the last straw. He agreed to help the North West Company drive away the Selkirk settlers.

"Half Breeds Travelling" by *Paul Kane*. For many years, Cuthbert Grant led the annual Métis buffalo hunt. Grant may still have been captain of the hunt when Paul Kane painted this picture.

Grant soon became the captain-general of the Métis. He led his people in raids against the Selkirk settlement. In 1816, he gathered 60 Métis to have it out with the settlers once and for all.

Grant planned to stop supplies from reaching the Selkirk colony. He was leading his Métis past the colony to a meeting-place when some of the settlers saw him and thought he was attacking. A group of them, led by Robert Semple, rushed out on foot to stop him.

Grant's men outnumbered the settlers and quickly surrounded them. Grant sent one of his men, François Boucher, forward to talk to the settlers. Semple angrily grabbed the bridle of Boucher's horse, and Boucher dismounted. One of Semple's men thought Boucher was attacking, and fired his gun. Suddenly, everyone was firing guns. When the smoke cleared, most of the settlers were dead.

Grant was unable to stop the killing, but he did all he could to protect the survivors. That night, he slept at the settlers' fort to protect the women and children of the colony. He helped the colonists leave peacefully and escorted them part way himself.

Grant was arrested for his part in the Battle of Seven Oaks, but he was not convicted. In 1821, the Hudson's Bay Company took over the North West Company. The Company's new leader was impressed by Grant's intelligence. He made Grant "Warden of the Plains" to enforce the Company's trading laws.

In 1823, Grant founded Grantown, a Métis town on the banks of the Assiniboine River. The Métis of Grantown became known as the Plains Rangers, a highly skilled force of buffalo hunters.

Under Grant's leadership, the Plains Rangers kept the Sioux Indians from invading the Red River lands. Grant and his Métis were now the defenders of the same colony they had once tried to destroy.

Leader of the Saulteaux

Chief Peguis listened angrily to the insults of Archibald McLeod. It was a hot June day in 1816, at the height of the fur trade wars. On the other side of the Red River, McLeod and other Nor'Westers had just driven the Selkirk settlers from their homes.

Chief Peguis had always been a good friend to the Selkirk settlers. Now McLeod had come to rage at him for helping the enemies of the North West Company.

Chief Peguis' eyes grew dark with contempt. Scornfully, he dismissed McLeod without a word. He was not about to desert the Selkirk settlers. Already that day, he had sent them food and arranged to bury their dead.

Chief Peguis was a powerful, imposing man with the deep, rich voice of an orator. He was a strong leader, and he ruled his young warriors with an iron hand.

Chief Peguis felt only pity for the sick and weary Scottish newcomers. Over the years, he had saved their lives many times over. When the settlers had run out of food, Peguis had led them to Pembina and taught them to hunt buffalo. Many of the children had been too weak for the 100-kilometre trek. Peguis' braves had lifted them onto their horses and carried them to safety.

In 1817, Lord Selkirk came to Red River in person. He thanked Peguis for all his help and presented him with many gifts. Peguis liked the "Silver Chief," as he called Selkirk. He agreed to grant the settlers land by a formal agreement.

On July 18, Peguis and four other chiefs gathered to discuss the terms of treaty with Lord Selkirk. The settlers were to receive a strip of land on both sides of the Red River. The Indians agreed to accept a gift of tobacco as a goodwill token for the moment. The next year, Selkirk would return with more goods to set a fairer price.

This was the first treaty between the British and the western Indians. Peguis signed it by drawing the mark of his totem animal.

Peguis held to the terms of the treaty and continued to help and protect the Selkirk settlers. However, as time passed, he and the other chiefs began to feel cheated. Lord Selkirk died in Europe before returning with a fairer price for the land. The Indians still only received some tobacco every year.

In his last years, Chief Peguis became a strong spokesman for Native rights. In 1861, when he was nearly 90, he and his son, Red Eagle, wrote an "Indian Manifesto" to lay out their land claims.

After Peguis died, his children and grandchildren went on working for Native rights. In 1871, Chief Red Eagle signed the new treaty that Peguis had worked for.

In the early 1800s, Britain still kept a tight rein on Upper and Lower Canada. A British governor ruled each of the colonies. He usually appointed the richest, most powerful colonists to help him rule in the Executive and Legislative Councils. The rest of the colonists could only elect people to the Legislative Assembly, which had no real power.

"Troops Conducting Prisoners in Canada." The prisoners in the cart are rebels who fought with *William Lyon Mackenzie*. Some of the rebels were hanged, and others deported to Australia. Later, most of them were pardoned.

The powerful men in the Executive and Legislative Councils held their positions for life. They told the governor how they wanted him to rule, and he usually followed their advice. These men controlled almost every aspect of life in the colonies. In Upper Canada, this ruling group was called the "Family Compact." In Lower Canada, it was called the "Château Clique."

In both the Canadas, people began to speak out against the Compact and the Clique. At first, the reformers worked for peaceful change. They wanted a government that would carry out the wishes of all the people.

As the years passed, few changes took place. The Family Compact and the Château Clique refused to give up their power. By the 1830s, some people began to talk of changing the government by force.

In November 1837, rebellion in Lower Canada broke out. Under *Louis-Joseph Papineau*, thousands of French Canadian "Patriotes" rose up angrily against their British rulers. After a month of fierce fighting, the Patriotes were defeated. However, their rebellion did loosen the Château Clique's hold on its power.

In Upper Canada, *William Lyon Mackenzie* also organized an armed revolt. In December 1837, he led a group of rebels toward Toronto's City Hall. Mackenzie's rebels were soon defeated, and many of them were forced to flee. However, they too managed to weaken the power of the men who ruled them.

Feudal Laird of the Ottawa Valley

As chief of his ancient Scottish clan, Archibald called himself "The McNab." He came to Upper Canada in 1823 to escape debts in Scotland.

McNab got title to 32 000 hectares in the Ottawa Valley. He was supposed to give this land to Scottish settlers when they proved they would work on it. Instead, he tried to *sell* the settlers the land. He made them promise to pay a large sum of money after they were settled.

McNab then refused to give the settlers the supplies they needed. Without any food, the settlers faced great hardship. The men had to find work far from home, while their wives foraged in the woods to feed their hungry children.

As the years passed, the settlers got deeper and deeper into McNab's debt. He tricked them into promising to pay him rent for the rest of their lives. He began to act like a feudal lord, demanding complete obedience. Sometimes, if settlers stood up to him, he had them thrown in jail.

Over and over, the settlers complained to the government. However, McNab had a great many friends in the powerful Family Compact. The government ignored the settlers and gave McNab all he asked for.

As time went on, The McNab grew steadily worse. He raided the settlers' land for timber and sent sheriffs to collect his debts. He threw families out of their homes in the middle of winter, and burned their houses to the ground. The settlers came close to open revolt.

At last, in the 1840s, the Family Compact began to lose its power. The government looked into the settlers' complaints and found them all to be true. In 1843, after 20 years of tyranny, The McNab fled the country in disgrace.

Leader of the Family Compact

Young John Strachan worked hard and won a scholarship to college. When his father died, he took extra teaching jobs to support his studies.

In 1799, Strachan went to Kingston as a penniless tutor. A few years later, he became an Anglican clergyman and opened a school in Cornwall.

1 Strachan was soon teaching the sons of Upper Canada's richest and most powerful families. He taught them to think like "British gentlemen," and trained them to become the next rulers of Upper Canada.

2 Strachan was still poor when he married Ann McGill, a wealthy widow. After the wedding, he could afford to live like an aristocrat. When he moved to York (later Toronto), he built a large mansion and called it "The Palace."

3 Strachan was the rector of York when the Americans invaded in 1813. He stood up to the American general and stopped American soldiers from looting the town.

4 Strachan took a leading role in the politics of Upper Canada. He and other leaders, many of them old students, became known as the Family Compact. As Tories, they believed in the British way of life. They did not believe the people should rule themselves.

6 In 1827, he founded King's College, which later became the University of Toronto. In 1839, Strachan became the first Anglican bishop of Toronto.

5 Strachan tried to help the people of Upper Canada in the way he thought was best. He worked hard to improve the lives of the poor and the sick. He also fought for free education, though only for Anglican schools.

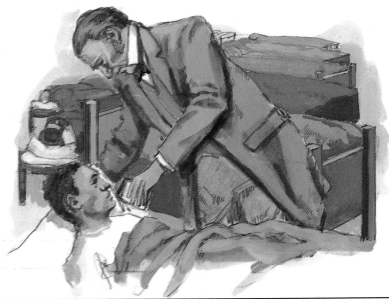

7 Strachan's views mellowed a bit as he grew older. By that time, the Family Compact had lost most of its power. Strachan was still bishop of Toronto when he died, at the age of 89.

Leader of the Patriotes

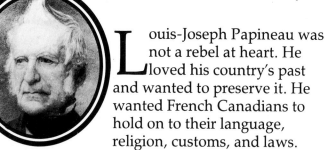

Louis-Joseph Papineau was not a rebel at heart. He loved his country's past and wanted to preserve it. He wanted French Canadians to hold on to their language, religion, customs, and laws.

Papineau disliked the new industries that took his people away from their farms. He disliked the canals that the British built to make money at his people's expense. Most of all, he disliked the British who ruled Lower Canada and owned most of its wealth.

Papineau was only 28 when he was elected to Lower Canada's Legislative Assembly. He was still under 30 when he became leader of the Parti Canadien and Speaker in the Assembly. At that time, the Assembly had very little power, although its members were elected by the people. The important decisions were all made by the Château Clique—the British governor and his English-speaking advisers.

In 1826, Papineau's Parti Canadien became the new Parti Patriote. The new party was more radical and took a firmer stand against the power of the Château Clique. In 1834, Papineau and Les Patriotes wrote a list of demands, called the Ninety-Two Resolutions. The most important demand was for a responsible government that followed the wishes of the people.

The British government refused to give the Patriotes the reforms they asked for. Papineau gave many outraged speeches. He started a boycott of British goods, to attack the British "in their most precious parts... their pocketbooks." He began wearing habitant clothing to the Assembly—a homespun coat and trousers, a knitted toque, and a red sash.

"Papineau Addressing A Crowd." Papineau tried to preach peace, but he was too late. The angry crowd wanted rebellion.

Les Patriotes began to call for more extreme measures. In Montreal, street-fighting broke out between French and British youths. Papineau did not want a violent rebellion, but by now he was powerless to stop it. His own passionate speeches moved his listeners toward open revolt.

In October 1837, Papineau urged an angry crowd at Saint-Charles to avoid violence. Then another leader cried out, "The time has come to melt down our tin spoons and plates into bullets." This is what the crowd wanted to hear. "Conquer or die!" rose the battle cry.

In early November, the British began to arrest Patriote leaders. Papineau avoided arrest and went to Saint-Denis, the rebel headquarters. He accepted command of the rebel forces, then went to his sister's house to avoid capture. The Patriotes wanted to make sure he was safe to lead Lower Canada if they won the war.

Within a few weeks, the rebels' dreams were shattered. After the British victory at Saint-Charles, Papineau knew the rebels had lost. He and other Patriote leaders slipped across the border to the United States. He spent the next eight years in poverty and exile, a defeated man.

Eventually the rebels were pardoned, and Papineau returned to Lower Canada. He was re-elected to the Assembly, but he was never really happy there again. After a few years, he decided to retire to his peaceful seigneury in the country.

"Rebels at Beauharnois." The artist, Katherine Ellice, was at Beauharnois and painted these rebels from memory. Her home was attacked and her father taken hostage.

Hero of Saint-Eustache

By early December 1837, the Patriote Rebellion was nearly over. *Louis-Joseph Papineau* and other Patriote leaders had already fled to the United States. Only in the county of Two Mountains, near Montreal, did the rebellion still live. There, a young doctor named Jean-Olivier Chénier waited to make a desperate last stand.

Here is the story of that last battle as one of Chénier's young followers might have told it.

"It was very cold the day Doctor Chénier first came to my father's farm. He sat in our kitchen, warming his hands by the fire. He told us we would always be poor until we drove out the British tyrants. He told us we must fight to win our freedom.

"A few weeks later, we heard that hundreds of men had gathered at Saint-Eustache. My cousin and I hurried to join them. Doctor Chénier was busy building barricades. He gave us shovels for weapons and told us to be brave.

"A week passed, and some of our men began to think twice about fighting. After all, they were only farmers armed with shovels and pitchforks. Then, on December 14, we heard that General Colborne was leading 2000 armed troops toward us. Many of our men rushed from the town in a panic.

"By the time the redcoats came into view, only 300 of us were left. Doctor Chénier led us across the frozen river to meet our enemy head on. The British charged us on their horses and drove us back to the stone church of Saint-Eustache.

"Doctor Chénier led us into the dark church and we barricaded the doors. Colborne's troops completely surrounded us. Somehow we held them off, firing from the narrow windows. Then a cannon shot blew in the door, and the British burst in. We ran up into the choir loft, destroying the stairs behind us.

"As we watched in horror, the British built a fire with wood from the altar. Soon, all the church was in flames around us. I clambered out the window and leapt to the churchyard below, as bullets exploded all around me.

"I looked up and saw Doctor Chénier try to escape. A bullet struck him as he leapt from the window, but he hardly seemed to notice. He landed on the frozen ground and began to run across the churchyard. Another bullet struck him through the heart, and he fell.

"The British did not show us any mercy. The soldiers went on a rampage, killing the helpless and wounded. The next day, they went on to Saint-Benoît and burned the village to the ground."

The Battle of Saint-Eustache was the largest of the Patriote Rebellion. Although the British won, the savage behaviour of their soldiers turned French Canada against them. The defeated Patriotes became heroes to their people. Their leader, Jean-Olivier Chénier, was hailed as a martyr of French Canada.

WILLIAM LYON MACKENZIE   1795–1861

The Rebel of Upper Canada

William Lyon Mackenzie came to Upper Canada from Scotland in 1820. He soon began to speak out against the power of the wealthy Tory families who controlled the province. In 1824, he started his own newspaper, the *Colonial Advocate*. He filled the paper with articles attacking the Tory government.

2 In 1828, Mackenzie was elected to Upper Canada's Assembly. His outspoken criticisms and hot-tempered speeches made him many enemies. In 1831, he was expelled from the Assembly by a Tory majority.

1 Mackenzie's articles out-raged the Tories. In 1826, a group of them raided his York office and smashed his press. When Mackenzie sued and won, he became a hero overnight.

3 The people of York re-elected Mackenzie by a vote of 119 to 1. With bagpipes skirling, he led a triumphant victory parade through the town. In the next two years, he would be expelled and re-elected four more times!

4 In 1834, Mackenzie became the first mayor of Toronto. The new city had many problems, including a cholera epidemic and muddy, overcrowded streets. Mackenzie worked hard, but many problems went unsolved.

5 Years passed, and the British refused to make reforms. In November 1837, Mackenzie heard about the Patriote Rebellion in Lower Canada. He decided to follow suit, and gathered 700 rebels at a tavern north of Toronto.

6 Mackenzie led his men down Yonge Street, but they were soon driven back. On December 7, the poorly-armed rebels were defeated by government militia. Mackenzie escaped to the United States and vainly tried to continue his fight.

7 After 12 years of exile, Mackenzie went back to Upper Canada. He was re-elected to the Assembly, where many reforms had now taken place. Mackenzie was as fiery as ever. He soon demanded a whole new set of changes!

BUILDING THE FUTURE

In the early 1800s, British North America was changing very quickly. Newcomers were pouring in from Britain, and towns and cities were springing up everywhere. In all the colonies, settlers were busy looking for ways to improve their lives.

As the settlements grew, they began to need new forms of transportation. In 1809, Canada's first steamship was launched on the St. Lawrence River. In 1816, the first through stagecoach run was started between Montreal and Kingston. In 1836, Canada's first railway was built, though large-scale railways were still in the future.

This was a time of great planning and building. Vast canal systems allowed ships to sail from the Atlantic right through the Great Lakes. In 1846, the first telegraph lines were laid between Toronto and Hamilton.

Other changes were also taking place. In all the colonies, people began to press for political change. In Upper and Lower Canada, colonists openly rebelled against direct rule by Britain. The rebellions failed, but they paved the way for many reforms that followed.

In the 1840s, the colonies at last won their battle for responsible government. In a responsible government, power is held by the representatives of the people. In the Canadas, Robert Baldwin and *Louis LaFontaine* ushered in the new system. In the Maritimes, *Joseph Howe* and Lemuel Wilmot led the battle for government reform.

"Canada's First Railway." The railway ran 23 km from Laprairie to St. Jean in Lower Canada. The entire trip took 45 minutes, amazingly quick for that time.

WILLIAM CARSON   1770–1843

Newfoundland's Fiery Reformer

In the early 1800s, Britain still ruled Newfoundland like a fishing station. A governor arrrived each spring with the fishing fleet and left in the fall when the season was over. The settlers had no government of their own to help them improve their lives. They had no schools, no roads, no hospitals, only their strong will to survive.

William Carson was a Scottish doctor who came to St. John's in 1808. He was appalled by the conditions he found there. Ramshackle wooden houses crowded around a muddy little track. Barefoot, ragged urchins played amidst heaps of rotting garbage.

Over the next years, Carson worked hard to improve conditions for the settlers. He wrote pamphlets to criticize the governor and attack British policy. He demanded that roads be built, and he helped to found Newfoundland's first hospital and library. He pressed the British to abolish unfair courts and to grant land to the settlers.

Carson also led the cry for representative government. In 1832, thanks largely to Carson, the settlers of Newfoundland voted for the first time. They elected Newfoundland's first House of Assembly to represent their concerns.

Carson was a fiery speaker and a stubborn, outspoken critic. In his long career, he made many powerful enemies. He was attacked in the newspapers, and lies were spread about him in the streets.

The more Carson was attacked, however, the more he dug in his heels. "To intolerance, to bigotry, and to tyranny I have a strong antipathy," he wrote. "And I find that it is returned."

Ship Master of the Atlantic

Samuel Cunard was the first Nova Scotian to head a huge international business empire. The son of a carpenter, Samuel was born and raised in Halifax. He showed early in life that he was determined to get on in the world.

2 As a young man, Samuel was fascinated by ships and the sea. He and his father set up a shipping company to trade with the United States and West Indies. When Abraham died in 1824, Samuel took over the company.

1 When he was a boy, Samuel grew vegetables and sold them at the market. He also knitted stockings for sale! His father, Abraham, expected everyone in the family to work hard.

3 Cunard found many ways to make ocean travel safer. He invented a system of light signals—green for starboard, red for port—that is still used today. He made sure that more lighthouses were built along the coast of Nova Scotia.

4 In 1833, the Canadian steamship *Royal William* became the first vessel to cross the Atlantic by steam power alone. Cunard was part owner of the ship. He knew that the future of ocean travel would depend on steam.

5 On July 4, 1840, Cunard left England aboard the steamship *Brittania*. He had just won the first contract to carry mail from Britain to North America by steam. Now he had to prove that his ship was as swift and reliable as he had promised.

6 After just 12 days, the *Brittania* docked at Halifax. Cunard expected a rousing welcome, but the ship had arrived two days *early*! The *Brittania* went on to Boston, where huge crowds had gathered to celebrate "Cunard Festival Day."

7 Sir Samuel Cunard died 25 years after the *Brittania*'s historic voyage, but his company lived on. In later years, the Cunard Line launched such famous luxury liners as the *Queen Mary* and the *Queen Elizabeth*.

Brewmaster and Shipbuilder

> This day bought eight bushels of barley, my commencement on the great stage of this world.
>
> from *The Journal of John Molson*

John Molson was full of big ideas when he came to Lower Canada at the age of 18. He soon began his first business, a small brewery on Montreal harbour. Just as he hoped, this business turned out to be the first of many.

Young Molson knew that to sell his beer he would have to make friends with his habitant customers. He learned to speak fluent French, and he bought a knitted toque, a homespun jacket, and homespun trousers. When the habitant farmers came to town to sell their grain, they found him smiling and dressed like one of themselves.

The farmers liked the eager young Scotsman and called him *le père* Molson. He charmed the farmers into selling him all their best grain. When he found out they grew little barley, he imported some himself and taught them how to raise it.

Molson was a good brewmaster, and his business thrived. He made so much money that he began to look for new ways to invest it.

In 1809, Molson launched the first steamship on the St. Lawrence River. This was a 26-metre paddle-wheeler called the *Accommodation*. The *Accommodation* could travel from Montreal to

Quebec City in only 36 hours. Until then, the trip had often taken as long as seven days!

Molson soon followed the *Accommodation* with other steamships. He set up a regular service between Montreal and Quebec.

Molson built many Montreal landmarks, including a theatre, a bank, a church, and a luxury hotel. He helped sponsor Canada's first railway, which ran between Laprairie and St. Jean, Quebec. He also served in Lower Canada's legislature, where he became known as "Judge Molson."

EGERTON RYERSON   1803–1882

"Free Education for All"

Suppose you were growing up in Upper Canada in the early 1800s. Most likely, you would never have the chance to go to school. Your parents would have no money to pay a teacher.

If you were lucky, you might go to a one-room log schoolhouse. You would sit on a rough bench and share a few worn-out books with the other students. You would practise writing on a stone slate, and do without paper, ink, blackboards, or maps. Your teacher would not know much more than you. After one or two years of this, your schooldays would be over.

Egerton Ryerson hated this system of education. As a young Methodist preacher, he travelled all over Upper Canada on horseback. He was appalled at the ignorance and the poverty he found. He knew that people could never improve their lives without proper schooling.

At that time, Upper Canada was ruled by a group of wealthy men called the Family Compact. Ryerson began to criticize the Compact and demand free education for all children. He wrote articles in the newspaper demanding government reforms.

In the 1840s, the Family Compact began to lose its power. Ryerson became Superintendent of Education for the province. First, he spent a year travelling through Europe to see how other countries taught their children. Then he spent the next 30 years making the changes he felt were needed.

Ryerson built fine new schools, complete with blackboards, maps, and supplies. He started teachers' schools, so that teachers would be properly trained. He got the government to pass laws to make sure all students got a free education. He imported textbooks, opened libraries, and encouraged students to learn far more than reading, writing, and arithmetic.

Ryerson's system was a great success. He lived long enough to see his schools become a model for education all over Canada.

The Reforming Governor

James Bruce, Earl of Elgin came to Canada as British governor in 1847. He believed Canadians were ready to rule themselves in a responsible government.

In 1848, the Reform Party took power from the Tories in a landslide election. They began to make changes to create a responsible government. Then *Louis LaFontaine* introduced the Rebellion Losses Bill to reimburse French Canadians who had suffered in the Papineau Rebellion.

The outraged Tories urged Elgin to stop the bill. They accused the Reformers of trying to give money to French traitors and rebels. Lord Elgin refused to interfere and the bill was passed. This proved that responsible government had come to Canada at last.

As Elgin's carriage left Parliament House, angry Tories pelted it with rocks and garbage. That night, 1500 Tories attacked Parliament House and set its rooms on fire. In the next months, they threw vegetables and dead rats at Elgin whenever he appeared.

Through all this turmoil, Elgin stayed calm and firm. Many people offered to fight the rioters, but Elgin refused to meet violence with violence. At last he withdrew to his country estate to let the fighting die down by itself.

Lord Elgin stayed on as governor of Canada for five more years. With his help, Tories began to work with Reformers, and French alongside British. Soon all these groups would join together to form the Dominion of Canada.

"The Burning of the Montreal Parliament." Tory rebels set fire to the parliament building and kept firemen from putting out the blaze. They stopped only to rescue a portrait of Queen Victoria from the flames.

SIR LOUIS LAFONTAINE   1807–1864

French Canada's Great Reformer

Louis LaFontaine was a Patriote, but he did not believe in violence. All his life, he had longed for the day when French Canadians would rule themselves. Before the Patriote Rebellion, he had stood proudly beside *Louis Papineau* in the Assembly. However, he would not take up arms, not even for Papineau.

After the Rebellion of 1837, most of the Patriotes went into exile. LaFontaine stayed behind to work peacefully for change. Over the next years, he pushed through many needed reforms. When Lower Canada was joined to Upper Canada, LaFontaine protected French Canadian rights. He worked with Robert Baldwin to take power away from the wealthy British Tories and give it to the ordinary people.

In 1848, LaFontaine and Baldwin were both premiers in a joint Assembly full of Reformers. LaFontaine felt the time had come to heal the wounds of the Patriote Rebellion. He had already made sure that the rebels were pardoned. Now he asked for £100 000 for the innocent French Canadians who had suffered at British hands.

The Assembly agreed, and the British governor, Lord Elgin, accepted their decision as law. This meant that Canada now had a responsible government. From now on, it would be run by the elected representatives of the people.

The English-speaking Tories were outraged. They knew they had lost control of the province. That very night, they burned the Parliament House of Montreal to the ground. The next day, they went to LaFontaine's house and smashed it

to pieces. They rioted for four months and assaulted LaFontaine twice in the street.

Through it all, LaFontaine stayed calm. He refused to meet violence with violence and did not call out the militia. Gradually, the rioting petered out by itself. When they calmed down, the Tories realized they had only hurt themselves. They had turned the man they hated, Louis LaFontaine, into a hero of his people.

NAVVIES ON THE RIDEAU

HOW THEY LIVED

Michael O'Reilly climbed up from the ship and looked around him at Montreal's busy harbour. He could hardly believe his long journey was over. The ship had been jammed with people, and most of the food had been rotten. Many of the passengers had been horribly sick with cholera.

Michael stretched his long arms and took a deep breath. Then he picked up his bag and followed the other passengers away from the pier.

Michael was only 18, but he was strong and eager to work. Back in Ireland, his family barely scraped a living from their landlord's fields. Michael wanted to save enough money to bring all his family to Canada.

Michael had heard on the ship that workers, or "navvies," were needed to build the Rideau Canal. The canal was to link the lakes and rivers between the Ottawa River and Lake Ontario. Then ships would be able to sail from the Atlantic Ocean through to the Great Lakes.

Within a few days, Michael signed on to help build the canal. Soon he was doing work that was very hard and dangerous.

One day Michael's team spent the whole day drilling a deep hole in a cliff face. They filled the hole with gunpowder, packed it down, and then set a fuse. The whole mass of limestone shook, and the rock shattered into thousands of pieces. One of the navvies was killed in the blast.

Michael's crew spent days hauling away the rubble by wheelbarrow. After that, they attacked the cliff with pick and shovel. Sometimes, as they dug, underground springs flooded the space where they worked.

In the fall, Michael's crew was sent to clear a wide area of bush and swamp. The navvies cut down hundreds of huge trees. The work was hardest in the swamplands. The swamps gave off a horrible stench like rotting meat. Mosquitoes

and flies swarmed in the thousands. Many of the navvies fell ill with a deadly sickness called "swamp fever."

Michael had no idea how cold he could be until his first winter in Canada. In December, he and some other men were surveying deep in the woods for a dam. The swampy ground was frozen and covered in deep snow.

The men surveyed in the daytime, working quickly to keep warm. At night they slept on hemlock branches with their feet almost in the fire. Michael and the others took turns drinking tea, because there was only one tin cup. They ate salt pork, which they thawed out over the fire.

One night the men sat around the fire, passing a cup of hot tea among them. Suddenly a thought struck Michael. "Did we miss Christmas?" he asked. The men fell silent, then began to laugh. Christmas had come and gone, while they shivered in the middle of a frozen swamp.

Voice of Nova Scotia

Joseph Howe was born in Halifax, Nova Scotia, the son of Loyalist parents. When he was 13, he had to leave school and work in his father's printing shop. "My books are few," he wrote, "but then the world is before me—a library open to all."

When he was 23, Howe bought a newspaper, *The Novascotian*. He soon used it to criticize the province's government, which was run by a handful of wealthy men.

2 Howe grew more and more critical of the government. He printed an unsigned letter that accused police and judges of corruption. He was arrested for libel and told that his case was hopeless.

1 Howe travelled all over Nova Scotia drumming up readers for his paper. He got to know the people and wrote about the things that mattered to them. Soon "Joe Howe" was welcome wherever he went.

3 Because no lawyer would take his case, Howe defended himself. He spoke for over six hours, passionately attacking the government. The crowds began to cheer as the jury set him free. For two days, people celebrated in the streets.

4 Howe made many enemies with his demands for reform. He won two duels, then refused to fight any more. He claimed that "a live editor is more useful than a dead hero."

6 In 1847, Howe led the Reformers to victory. They set up the first government in British North America to represent the wishes of the people. Howe had won responsible government without "a blow struck or a pane of glass broken."

5 In 1836, Howe was elected to the Legislative Assembly. Over the next years, he worked tirelessly for reforms. He quarrelled with the British governor and forced the British to send a replacement.

7 Howe continued to fight for the things he believed in. Years later, he fought against union with Canada because he thought it would ruin Nova Scotia's economy. When he could not stop Confederation, he insisted on better terms.

As the years passed, British North Americans began to grow more sure of themselves. Canals were dug, industries boomed, and the people demanded greater freedom.

Slowly, the colonists stopped thinking of themselves as French or British. In each of the provinces, they found new identities. They were "Bluenoses" from Nova Scotia, "Patriotes" from Lower Canada, or "Plains Rangers" from the Red River lands in the West.

As the colonists grew stronger, their arts began to surge into life. "Pioneer arts," such as quilting and woodcarving, continued to flourish. Printing presses became easier to build, and newspapers and magazines began to spring up. In the 1840s, the first photographs were taken.

Each of the colonies began to find its own special voice. In Nova Scotia, *Thomas Haliburton* wrote comic stories to make the settlers laugh at themselves. In Lower Canada, *François-Xavier Garneau* inspired his readers with the glorious past of New France.

In Upper Canada, *Susanna Moodie* wrote about the joys and trials of pioneer life. In the West, *Paul Kane* sketched Native chiefs, while *Pierre Falcon* turned the adventures of the Métis into song.

In stories, poems, and paintings, all these artists told of life in a new land. With this new blossoming of the arts, British North America began to come of age.

"The Pigeon Hunt." The artist, Antoine Plamondon, was the first Quebec painter to study in France. He mixed classical techniques with down-to-earth themes to produce a truly "Quebec" style of painting.

Creator of Sam Slick

Here's a book they've namesaked arter me, Sam Slick, the Clockmaker. . . . It wipes up the Bluenoses considerable hard, and don't let off the Yankees so very easy either, but it's generally allowed to be about the prettiest book ever writ in this country.

Sam Slick, in *The Clockmaker*

Thomas Haliburton was born and raised in Windsor, Nova Scotia. His family were Loyalists and taught him to love the British way of life. He made the most of his wealth and success, and he enjoyed living well.

Haliburton thought Nova Scotians, or "Bluenoses," should be happy to be ruled by Britain. Instead of complaining, they should get on with developing their farms, lumber mills, and shipyards. Otherwise, they would soon lose out to the enterprising Yankees.

Haliburton invented Sam Slick to get across these views in a comic way. Sam was a Yankee pedlar who travelled all over Nova Scotia selling his clocks. He poked fun at the Bluenoses he met, and called them lazy.

Haliburton also used Sam Slick to make fun of the Yankees. Sam was fast-talking, self-serving, conceited, and a little dishonest. Haliburton thought all these traits were American.

Sam had a way with words, and many of his "wise saws" are still used today. It was Sam who

"I am Sam Slick, says I."

This is one of the drawings from Haliburton's *The Clockmaker*, featuring Sam Slick.

first said that "the early bird gets the worm." He was the first to call someone a "stick-in-the-mud" or to laugh at a person for "barking up the wrong tree."

Sam Slick became very popular, and many more stories were written about him. Meanwhile, Thomas Haliburton became Canada's first internationally famous writer.

Lost Voice of the Beothuks

starved. Others died of diseases brought by the newcomers. Sometimes Europeans killed them for sport. By 1800, there were only a few Beothuks left alive.

In 1823, Shawnawdithit was captured along with her mother and sister. Shawnawdithit was a handsome young woman, with a quick mind and a lovely smile. Her warmth and friendliness soon won over her British captors, who called her Nancy. They gave her a pencil and paper, and with one fluid stroke she drew them a perfect picture of a deer.

In the early 1800s, a lonely young woman, Shawnawdithit, tried to describe her way of life to her British captors. Much of what we know about the Beothuk Indians of Newfoundland is based on her words and drawings.

From the start, European settlement was a disaster for the Beothuks. In 1612, a seaman named John Guy feasted and traded with the Beothuks at Trinity Bay. The next spring, an armed fishing boat pulled into the bay. The Beothuks thought it was Guy and gathered in excitement to welcome him. The boat's captain thought the Indians were attacking, so he opened fire on them.

From then on, the Beothuks fled from Europeans on sight. As Newfoundland settlements spread, the Beothuks lost their hunting and fishing grounds. Many of them

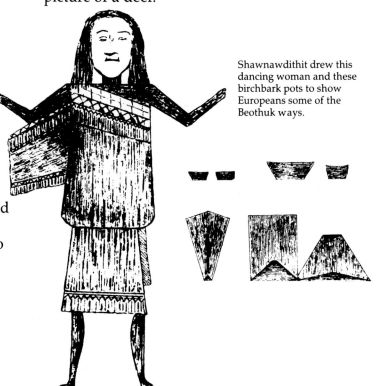

Shawnawdithit drew this dancing woman and these birchbark pots to show Europeans some of the Beothuk ways.

The settlers decided to send the Beothuks back to their people. They took the three women to the shore of the Bay of Exploits and left them. Shawnawdithit's mother and sister had become very ill, so she set off alone to look for her people. After a long and fruitless search, she finally gave up hope.

Shawnawdithit returned to her mother and sister, and began to lead them to the nearest British settlement. The two sick women died on the trek. Shawnawdithit carried on alone.

In the years that followed, Shawnawdithit worked as an unpaid servant in the home of a British family. She cooked and scrubbed and washed, and played with the family's small children. Sometimes she carved beautiful ornaments from wood and deer bone. Other times, she slipped off alone to the forest.

By 1827, Newfoundland settlers had begun to sympathize with the plight of the Beothuks. An explorer, William Epp Cormack, went on a long journey to try to bring them aid. When he found no trace of the Beothuks, he realized Shawnawdithit might be the last of her people.

Cormack brought Shawnawdithit into his home to learn as much as he could from her. She drew him pictures to show him how the Beothuks had hunted and worshipped. She told him the tragic history of her people. She told how they had dwindled down to her mother, sister, and a few others. Starving, they had headed for the coast, where they had scattered or been captured.

Shawnawdithit was already very ill when she told Cormack the story of the Beothuks. She died in the spring of 1829, of tuberculosis. With her death, an entire people were lost to the world forever. No other Beothuk Indian was ever seen alive.

Preserver of Past Glories

François-Xavier Garneau was proud of French Canada's traditions. He loved to stroll down Quebec City's cobbled streets, remembering those who had walked there before him. Under British rule, French Canadians had lost touch with their heroic past. Garneau decided to restore his people's pride in their history.

2 Because his family was poor, Garneau had to leave school at 14. He became a clerk and started to educate himself by reading books. He saved money for a trip to Europe, where he met many artists and scholars.

3 Back in Quebec City, Garneau became involved in politics. He worked on *Le canadien*, a newspaper that supported *Papineau* and the Patriotes.

1 As a boy, Garneau loved to hear about his country's past. His grandfather told him exciting stories about the battles he had seen in the Seven Years War.

4 In 1839, the British governor, Lord Durham, called French Canadians "a people with no history and no literature." Garneau was outraged, and set out to prove Durham wrong.

6 In the *History of Canada*, Garneau brought the colourful past of French Canada to life. The book was a great success and gave French Canadians a new pride in their heritage.

5 Garneau began to write a history of French Canada, starting with the voyages of *Jacques Cartier*. He still worked at a daytime job, so he wrote at night when his family was asleep. When he finished, his book was 1600 pages long!

7 Garneau became a leader of the arts in French Canada and inspired other artists to preserve their culture. When Quebec became a province of Canada, it took for its motto, "Je me souviens," or "I remember."

The Unhappy Pioneer

"My love for Canada," wrote Susanna Moodie, "was a feeling very like that which a condemned criminal feels for his cell."

Susanna and her husband, John Moodie, came to Upper Canada to make a better life for themselves. They were bitterly disappointed when they found how hard they would have to work just to stay alive.

In England, Susanna had been a gentlewoman, with servants to do her work for her. In Canada, she found herself milking cows and making her own soap from lye. She was tormented by heat and black flies, and driven half-mad by the endless winters. Three times, her house caught fire. Once, it burned right to the ground.

During one bad time, Susanna and John lay ill for weeks with fever. Their little girl was also sick, and they had a newborn baby son. They listened helplessly to the cries of their children, far from medical help.

Through these hard years, Susanna eased her despair by writing down her thoughts. She wrote poems like this one, about the loneliness of her backwoods life:

> And silence—awful silence broods
> Profoundly o'er these solitudes;
> Not but the lapsing of the floods
> Breaks the deep stillness of the woods;
> A sense of desolation reigns
> O'er these unpeopled forest plains...

As time passed, Susanna began to make money with her writing. She worked late at night, after the children were asleep. For a lamp, she used twisted rags dipped in oil. Sometimes, she could not even afford to mail her manuscripts to be published.

Susanna's books became popular in England. She had a witty, colourful style, and a gift for making her eccentric characters come alive. The most famous book was *Roughing It in the Bush*, which told about her own pioneer experiences. Susanna wrote this book to discourage well-born people like herself from settling in Canada.

After Susanna's writing began to sell, she left her backwoods life to settle in Belleville. To her surprise, she found that she had come to love her pioneer home. She had learned many valuable lessons there in courage and survival.

A hundred years later, another Canadian writer wrote about Susanna's life as a pioneer. Margaret Atwood was fascinated by Susanna's mixed feelings of love and hate for the land.

Here are some lines from Margaret Atwood's poem, "Thoughts from Underground." In the poem, Susanna Moodie is remembering her past.

In winter our teeth were brittle
with cold. We fed on squirrels.
At night the house cracked.
In the morning, we thawed
the bad bread over the stove.

Then we were made successful
and I felt I ought to love
this country.
　　　　　I said I loved it
and my mind saw double.

Painter of a Vanishing World

Paul Kane looked around him sadly at the streets of Toronto. He had come back to the city after years of studying art in Europe. Nothing seemed the same to him. Once, hundreds of Mississauga Indians had walked through the streets, going about their business. Now, it seemed, the Indians had gone elsewhere.

Kane remembered the words of George Catlin, an American painter he had met in London. "The duty of a North American artist is to paint the disappearing cultures of the Native Peoples." Now Kane saw how quickly North America was changing. He decided to leave at once on a journey into the wilderness.

> To me the wild woods were not entirely unknown, and the Indians recalled old friends with whom I had associated in my childhood. . . . The principal object in my undertaking was to sketch pictures of the principal chiefs and their original costumes, to illustrate their manners and customs, and to represent the scenery of an almost unknown country.

from *Wanderings of an Artist among the Indians of North America*, by Paul Kane

In 1845, Kane left on his first trip. He spent time with the Indians near Lake Huron, studying and sketching their way of life. He turned back after he reached Sault Ste. Marie.

The next year, Kane left on a much longer journey. Armed with his gun, sketchbook, and paints, he set off alone for the far Canadian West.

"Indian Encampment on Lake Huron" by Paul Kane. The easy rhythm of camp life appealed to Kane. Wherever he went, Indian tribes made him feel welcome.

"Assiniboine Hunting Buffalo" by Paul Kane. Kane went along on several buffalo hunts. Once he was so busy sketching that he fell off his horse in front of a charging buffalo.

During the next three years, Kane lived a life of high adventure. He travelled on foot, on snowshoe, on horseback, and by canoe. He shot rapids with fur traders, and ran buffalo with the Métis on the prairies. He wandered through forests, across plains, over mountains, and up rivers. He made it all the way to "Vancouver's Island" and back again.

Through his travels, Kane met thousands of Native people. He was an easygoing man and made friends wherever he went. He sketched hundreds of Indians, along with their clothing, homes, ceremonies, and art forms. He was especially drawn to the Pacific Coast tribes, and he was one of the first to study their ways.

Kane returned to Toronto with over 700 sketches of the Western Indians and their lands. From them, he made a series of huge, colourful paintings that were landmarks in Canadian art. Yet it is Kane's sketches, not his paintings, that are most loved today. In fresh, clear strokes, they capture a West that now is only a memory.

Kane was an old man before the importance of his work began to be recognized. This praise must have been sweet to him, for he could no longer paint. During his travels through the West, snow blindness had badly damaged his eyes.

Bard of the Métis

And now, my friends, come on!
Raise your glasses everyone!
A toast to this fine song
And its maker, Pierre Falcon!

from *General Dickson*,
by Pierre Falcon

He was a fiery little man, quick-moving and agile. His eyes were dark and merry, and his hair hung to his shoulders, Red River style. He felt happiest with a fiddle in his arm, making up songs about his people, the Métis.

Pierre Falcon lived through many of the Métis' most exciting years on the plains. "Pierre the Rhymer" was at the Battle of Seven Oaks, when the Métis clashed with a group of Scottish settlers. He wrote a song about the battle that very night, to celebrate the Métis victory.

In his songs, Pierre the Rhymer tried to catch the flavour of the world around him. Sometimes he made up stirring songs that praised the Métis as warriors. Sometimes he sang about exciting adventures, like the great Métis buffalo hunt. Sometimes he made up comic songs that poked fun at the Métis and their enemies alike.

Pierre Falcon's songs were loved by people all through the West. The Métis sang them as they rode their horses across the prairie. The voyageurs sang them in their canoes or around their campfires. The fur traders sang them at the great feasts in their forts.

During his lifetime, Pierre the Rhymer saw his people hailed as lords of the prairie. Then, as he grew old, he saw them struggle to keep their way of life. Pierre Falcon was 77 when he made up his last song. He sang about the Red River Rebellion and its leader, Louis Riel.

La Bataille des Sept Chênes

Would you like to hear me sing
Vou-lez vous é-cou-ter chan-ter

Of — a true and re-cent thing?
U-ne chan-son de vé-ri-té?

On June nine-teenth, the brave Bois Bru-lés
Le dix-neuf de juin, la bande des Bois Bru-lés

Rode like war-riors and w-on the day.
Sont ar-ri-vés commes des bra-ves guer-riers.

Chapter Six

FROM SEA TO SEA
1850 - 1867

The Bustling Colonies
James Barry
Sir Casimir Gzowski
Abigail Becker
Thomas Keefer
Abraham Gesner
The Saint John Four

North to Freedom
Mary Ann Shadd
Josiah Henson
Anne-Marie Weems

Settling the West
Maskepetoon
John Palliser
James McKay
Sir James Douglas
Sylvia Stark

Gold!
Catherine Schubert
Billy Barker
Cariboo Cameron
Matthew Baillie Begbie
Gold Seekers from China

The Roof of the World
Kridlak
Sir John Franklin
John Rae
Ipilkvik and Tukkolerktuk

Words and Pictures
Mary Jane Katzmann
Cornelius Krieghoff
Octave Crémazie
Philippe-Joseph Aubert de Gaspé
William Hind
Humphrey Lloyd Hime

One Canada
Sir Samuel Leonard Tilley
Sir John A. Macdonald
Sir Charles Tupper
Sir Georges-Etienne Cartier
George Brown
Thomas D'Arcy McGee

THE BUSTLING COLONIES

In the mid-1800s, British North America exploded with new ideas and new inventions. The first oil wells were drilled, the first photos taken, and the first railway tracks laid. New inventions, such as sewing machines, cut out hours of work in the home. In the fields, new mowers and reapers changed work methods forever.

Perhaps the most important changes were those that linked the colonies together. Telegraph cables spread across the countryside, connecting remote settlements to larger centres. Canals were dug, bridges were built, and "railway fever" swept the land. Soon, the "Iron Horse" ran to many of the colonies' eastern cities and towns.

With all this hustle and bustle, British North Americans began to take new pride in themselves. Victorious athletes, such as the *Saint John Four*, became sports heroes across the land. The brave deeds of people like *Abigail Becker* became legends overnight. In the East, the great Maritime sailing ships were the pride of every man, woman, and child.

As the colonies grew stronger, they began to draw closer together. Many colonists began to speak of coming together in one great union. Separately, the colonies had already achieved a great deal. In unity, they might find the strength to achieve more.

"Submarine Cable Linking Europe with North America." The Atlantic telegraph cable ran under the ocean between Britain and Newfoundland. It was first proposed by Fred Gisborne, a Maritime inventor and engineer.

Canada's First Woman Doctor

She was an intense young girl, with a quick mind and a burning wish to serve the world as a doctor. However, at that time, British women could not even study at university, much less practise medicine. The young girl could see only one way to have the career she wanted. She would change her name to "James" and disguise herself as a boy!

Over the years, Dr. Barry's disguise must have been very hard to keep up. She could never have any close friends in case they guessed her secret. She could never fall in love or have a normal family life.

Dr. James Barry became an army surgeon and travelled all over the world. In South Africa, she performed one of the first Caesarean births in which mother and baby both lived. She spoke out against the terrible conditions in the leper colonies, prisons, and insane asylums. She made enemies with her criticisms, and once she even fought a duel.

In 1857, Dr. Barry came to Montreal as inspector-general of Canada's military hospitals. This was the highest medical post in the country. Right away, she set to work improving health conditions for the army. She insisted that troops be fed well and given clean living quarters.

James Barry's lonely life made her a true eccentric. She decorated her uniform with fancy epaulets and wore cocked hats with long, feathery plumes. She loved to ride through Montreal wrapped in rich furs in a fine red sleigh with silver

"Dr. Barry in Jamaica." The little dog in this photo was only one in a long line of white lapdogs. Dr. Barry called all of them "Psyche."

bells. Everywhere she went, she took along her white lapdog, Psyche.

James Barry kept her secret right up to her death. For over 50 years, she lived in disguise as a man. Perhaps she was the first woman doctor in the world. She was certainly the first in Canada.

SIR CASIMIR GZOWSKI   1813–1898

The Gallant Engineer

Casimir Gzowski was the son of a Polish count. In 1830, when he was 17, he joined the army as an engineer. That same year, Polish patriots rebelled against their Russian rulers, and young Gzowski joined them.

1 The Polish patriots lost their rebellion. Pushed back to the Austrian border, they surrendered to the Austrian army. Later, they were exiled to North America.

2 Gzowski landed in New York as a poor Polish exile. He soon learned English and began working again as an engineer. In 1841, he moved to Upper Canada to work in the London District.

3 Gzowski organized the building of roads, bridges, and lighthouses. He ranged far and wide through the backwoods, and fell in love with the Ontario wilderness.

4 Gzowski used the most advanced designs for his bridges and roads. Many people thought his new bridge at London looked too weak. Gzowski stood under the bridge himself while a battery of heavy artillery crossed over it.

6 In 1853, Gzowski started his own railway-building company. The next year, he started work on the difficult Grand Trunk Railway. Every time a section was completed, a celebration was held.

5 Like many engineers, Gzowski soon caught "railway fever." He became chief engineer for the St. Lawrence and Atlantic Railway, and surveyed the entire route on foot.

7 In 1871, Gzowski began to build the International Bridge across the treacherous Niagara River. This was Gzowski's greatest engineering feat, the crowning glory of his great career.

Heroine of Long Point

It was late November, 1854. In the hours before dawn, a fierce winter gale raged across Lake Erie. Blinded by snow and sleet, the merchant schooner *Conductor* ran aground on the treacherous sandbars off Long Point. The ship shuddered and keeled over, and its eight crewmen climbed desperately up its rigging. They lashed themselves to the ship's masts, praying for a miracle to save them.

Luckily for the men, help was not far away. Abigail Becker, a brave young woman of 24, lived in a cabin on Long Point with her many children and stepchildren. Here is the story of Abigail's heroic rescue of the men. It is told through the eyes of Lee Hays, the *Conductor*'s 16-year-old cabin boy.

"All night and all morning, the blizzard swirled around us. We huddled together on a small platform near the top of the foremast. Our clothes were frozen stiff, and our hair and eyebrows were white with frost.

"Suddenly, the captain began to cheer. A tall young woman was striding across the beach, gathering driftwood to build a fire. Her long black hair whipped across her face in the wind as she beckoned toward us.

"We were hundreds of metres out from shore. All around us, the icy water broke in angry white-capped waves. Even in good weather, the undertow around Long Point could drag a strong swimmer far out from shore.

"'Look!' the first mate cried. 'She's coming for us!' The woman had left the shore and was wading out into the lake. With each step she shuddered as icy waves pounded against her

body. Soon she was up to her neck in foaming water.

"The captain stood up, peeled off his coat, and began to pull off his boots. 'Wait till I'm ashore,' he ordered. 'Then follow, one by one.' He grabbed a rope, swung out past the yard-arm, and let go.

"The woman struggled out to meet the captain, stretching forward her long arms. She almost had him when a huge wave swept both of them under. Somehow, she caught hold of him and pulled him up onto the beach.

"The first mate plunged into the waves, then the bos'n and the ship's carpenter. The woman met each one of them and dragged them through the icy waves to shore.

"At last it was my turn. By now it was almost dark again, and the rough waves looked black and terrifying. I grabbed the rope, swung clear of the ship, and took a deep gulp of air. Then I plunged down and down into the ice-cold water.

"I could feel the strong current pushing me from shore, so I began to swim with all my might. As the waves swept over me, I went under again and again. Finally I felt myself slip beneath the waves forever.

"Just at that moment, a powerful hand grabbed my arm. I coughed and spluttered as the woman heaved me over her shoulder. Icy waves crashed against us, but she never let go. At long last, she reached the shore and placed me in the arms of my captain."

When Abigail Becker rescued the sailors, she did not even know how to swim! Yet she was always surprised when people gave her medals or called her a heroine. "I only did my duty," she would say, "just as anyone else would have done."

219

The Water Engineer

Thomas Keefer grew up in Thorold, near the Niagara River. As a boy, he watched the workmen build the first Welland Canal. To young Keefer, the canal's engineers seemed like gods. These were men with the power to move mountains and change the course of rivers.

When Keefer grew older, he too learned how to blast through rock and divert rivers. When he was 17, he learned engineering by going to work on the Erie Canal. He soon made a name for himself as a skilled and talented engineer.

Keefer designed railways and built roads, but most of his work involved water. He built canals and timber slides to move lumber down the Ottawa River. He deepened the St. Lawrence channels and surveyed its rapids. He built bridges across rivers, and he built canals between them.

Keefer also built Canada's first public water systems. At that time, the cities had no clean water or sewage systems. Dead horses floated in the harbours of Toronto and Montreal. Wells were drilled next to outhouses, and open sewers ran through the muddy streets. Rats thrived, and people died in the thousands from typhoid and cholera.

Keefer built his first water works in Montreal. He built an aqueduct to bring fresh water to the city, and reservoirs to store it. He built pumps and underground pipes to send the water into homes and businesses.

The Montreal Water Works were a great success. Keefer began to plan public water systems for other cities. Over the next years, he helped build water works in Hamilton, Toronto, Ottawa, Halifax, London, and Quebec City. All over Canada, Keefer brought health and fresh, clean water into city homes.

ABRAHAM GESNER   1797–1864

The Lamplighter

Abraham Gesner was a Nova Scotian doctor who loved to study rocks and minerals. He became an expert on Maritime geology, and made the first geological surveys of Prince Edward Island and New Brunswick.

2 As the years passed, Gesner found little support for his work in the Maritimes. He went to New York and won a contract to light up the city streets. Soon people all over North America used kerosene in their lamps.

3 Gesner's success came to an end when a cheaper source of kerosene was found. He lost almost everything and returned to Nova Scotia. He died there soon after, still full of hopeful plans for the future.

1 In 1846, Gesner invented a new fuel for lamps. It gave a clear, smoke-free light, much brighter than whale-oil or candlelight. Gesner named his fuel "keroselain," or kerosene.

Canada's First Sports Heroes

In August 1867, many of the world's greatest artists, athletes, and scientists gathered in France for the great Paris Fair. The people of Saint John, New Brunswick, sent their finest rowing team to the Fair. The rowers were Robert

Fulton, George Price, Samuel Hutton, and Elijah Ross—the Saint John Four.

In Europe, rowing was considered a sport for young "gentlemen" of the upper classes. The uniforms were quiet and conservative, and the boats were delicate and finely crafted.

When the Saint John Four arrived in Paris, people laughed out loud at them. Canada's rowers were hardy working men—three fishermen and a lighthouse-keeper. They wore gaudy outfits with leather suspenders and bright pink caps. Their boats were crude, hand-made, and far heavier than the European models.

On the day of the boat races, everyone expected the Saint John Four to make fools of themselves. Some even accused them of dangerous rowing because they did not use a fifth person to steer.

A white flag dropped and the first race began. The crowd gasped as the Saint John Four shot into the lead. With swift, vigorous strokes, the Four kept easily ahead of their nearest rivals. They reached a buoy at the end of the course, and rounded it smoothly to win the return lap. Without a steersman, the Saint John Four could actually turn much faster!

In the second race, the Four went up against England's oldest and best rowing clubs. Once again they won the race easily. By now, the crowd adored them. One delighted reporter wrote that the Canadians had shown "the rest of the world how to row."

NORTH TO FREEDOM

The Underground Railroad didn't run
  on steam.
The Underground Railroad didn't run on
  coal.
The pounding you heard was a pulsing
  blood stream.
What made the Road run was the
  strength of the soul.

  Traditional

In the mid-1800s, thousands of Black men and women came to Canada to escape from slavery. These people had been forced to work all their lives for White "owners" in the American South. Most had picked cotton, sugar cane, or tobacco on large southern plantations.

Slavery was illegal in the northern United States, but escaped slaves were not safe there. Slave hunters combed the northern states for runaways, and collected rewards for taking them back to their owners. In British North America, however, slavery was illegal after 1833. Runaway slaves had the same rights as anyone else there.

Southern slaves began to hear of this free land to the north. Many escaped, risking their lives in the name of freedom. Some made their way alone, guided only by the North Star or the moss on the north side of trees. Most, however, had help from the Underground Railroad.

The Underground Railroad had nothing to do with trains. Its "conductors" were the many brave people, such as the Quakers, who broke the law to help escaped slaves. Conductors housed and fed

"The Underground Railroad" by Charles T. Webber. The term "underground railroad" was coined by a confused slave owner. When his slaves vanished, he decided they must have escaped on a train running beneath the ground.

the runaways, then guided them to the next person who would help them. The secret "railroad stations" were homes, barns, and churches where slaves could hide on their way north.

The ex-slaves found freedom in Canada, but some also found prejudice and poverty. Despite their hardships, however, many Black Canadians put down new roots deep in Canadian soil.

Crusader for Black Rights

It was a chilly Sunday afternoon, in Chatham, Canada West. A young boy ran barefoot through the empty streets, fleeing desperately from his pursuers. He was weak from hunger and exhaustion, and he began to lose ground. Then the slave-hunters caught up to him, and the boy cried out in terror.

Mary Ann Shadd heard the cry and ran out into the street. She strode angrily toward the slave-hunters. "You have no rights here," she told them. "This boy is free!"

The slave-hunters just laughed at her. They were large, menacing men, but Mary Ann was not afraid. She grabbed the boy and tore him away from the hunters. "Run!" she cried, taking his hand in hers.

Mary Ann ran with the frightened boy, the slave-catchers close behind them. Then she fixed her eyes on the door of the court-house. Dragging the boy behind her, she raced up the court-house steps and ran inside. "Ring the bell!" she gasped, slamming the door behind her.

The bell-ringer rang the bell so loudly that half the town came running. The slave-hunters watched in amazement as Mary Ann came out to the court-house steps. Tall and handsome, with flashing eyes and a stirring voice, she began to speak. The crowd grew quiet and listened closely to every word.

Mary Ann pointed to the slave-hunters and accused them of making money from the misery of her people. She told the crowd how the hunters had illegally chased a frightened child into Canada. She urged the people of Chatham to drive these villains from their midst.

As Mary Ann spoke, the townspeople grew more and more outraged. The slave-hunters began to grow alarmed. "Put them in jail!" cried someone. "Jail's too good for 'em!" called someone else. Soon the whole crowd was heading angrily toward the slave-hunters. The hunters turned and fled, feeling lucky to escape with their lives.

Mary Ann Shadd worked all her life to improve conditions for her people. She was born in freedom and came to Chatham as a child with her family. As a young woman, she devoted years to starting a school for Black children.

Time after time, Mary Ann spoke out strongly against prejudice and injustice. In 1853, she started a newspaper, *The Provincial Freeman*. In its pages, she waged her own war on bigotry and slavery.

The Provincial Freeman was a lively paper, full of salty humour and homespun wisdom. It printed news items on Black life in Canada and strong editorials in defence of Black rights. *The Freeman* gave the escaped slaves of Canada West a new sense of purpose and identity.

Like many other Black people, Mary Ann left Canada to fight against slavery in the American Civil War. After the war, she stayed in the United States and became one of its first woman lawyers.

For the rest of her life, Mary Ann Shadd went on working for Black rights. As a writer, teacher, lawyer, and speaker, she worked selflessly and tirelessly to improve the lives of her people.

Freedom-Seeker

I'm on my way to Canada
That cold and distant land,
The dire effects of slavery
I can no longer stand.
Farewell, old master,
Don't come after me.
I'm on my way to Canada
Where coloured men are free.

Traditional

"Josiah Henson and his wife, Charlotte."

Josiah Henson's first memories of slavery were grim and bitter. As a child, he saw his father's ear cut off for stopping a brutal assault on his mother. Then all the members of his family were sold to different owners. Henson never saw any of them again.

As a young man, Henson got married and began saving money to buy his way out of slavery. After many long years, he saved over $300, nearly enough for his freedom. His master took the money, then tried to sell him to another owner.

Henson decided the time had come to escape. He chose a dark moonless night in September 1830. He and his wife, Charlotte, gathered up all they had in the world—a small packet of food, 25¢, and the clothes on their back.

Henson put his two youngest children into a knapsack, then hoisted it onto his back. He led his family away from Kentucky, across the Ohio River to Indiana.

Henson and his family hid by day and tramped through woods by night. In Ohio, they found friends who fed them and steered them north to Canada.

For many long nights, the family struggled through dense bush, while wolves howled all around them. Soon they were hungry again, living on nothing but dried beef. Once a group of Indians took pity on them, and took them back to their village to rest.

"The Hensons Escape by Night." These engravings were used to illustrate the book Henson wrote to describe his escape.

When Henson reached Lake Erie, he had a stroke of luck. A gruff Scottish sea-captain hired him for a day, then took the family across the lake to New York. At Buffalo, the captain bought the Hensons' passage on a ferry across the Niagara River.

On October 28, 1830, Henson reached the Canadian shore. He threw himself on the ground, seized a handful of soil, and kissed it.

Henson soon found that, even in Canada, his people faced injustice. He began to dream of starting a self-supporting Black settlement. There, runaway slaves could clear farms, start up a lumber industry, and build better lives for their children.

Henson travelled all through New England and the Canadas, preaching against slavery and spreading his dream. In the late 1830s, he and other escaped slaves started the Dawn settlement (near present-day Dresden, Ontario). Although Dawn never completely lived up to Henson's dream, it gave many ex-slaves a new start in life.

In 1849, Henson wrote a small book, *The Life of Josiah Henson*, about his escape from slavery. A few years later, an American writer named Harriet Beecher Stowe also wrote about runaway slaves. Her book, *Uncle Tom's Cabin*, turned thousands of people against slavery. Many readers came to believe that "Uncle Tom" was based on Josiah Henson.

When Henson reached Canadian soil, he threw himself down on his knees and prayed.

A Young Freedom-Seeker

Anne-Marie Weems was born into slavery on a plantation in Maryland. When she was only 12, her mother and father were sold far away to a distant farm. She was left alone, with no family to protect her.

In time, Anne-Marie became friends with an old slave. He told her how to escape to Canada by following the North Star. He also told her how to find help in Washington, D.C.

When Anne-Marie was 15, she saw her chance to escape at last. Here is her story, as she herself might have told it.

"Early one morning, I crept into the supply house and gathered some food. That night I cut my hair and dressed up like a boy. Then, when everyone was asleep, I ran into the woods.

"It was a bright starry night, and I walked and walked. I knew the slave-hunters might already be after me. When day-break came, I stopped and hid in thick bushes.

"I stayed away from roads and struggled through dense woods and tangled undergrowth. I criss-crossed streams to throw the slave-hunters' bloodhounds off my trail.

"One morning I was awakened by the sound of men talking in deep voices. The men spoke my name, and said I was worth $500. They were slave-hunters, combing the woods with their hounds!

"I said a prayer, and pulled myself deeper into the bushes. Somehow they missed me and moved on. All that day, I stayed awake, listening for their return.

"I walked all night, as fast as I could, hardly stopping to rest. When morning came, I had reached the woods just outside Washington.

"That night, long after sunset, I stole into the city. I kept to the shadows and followed the directions the old slave had told me. At last I came to a big house with a picket fence, two willow trees, a white door, and a wide porch.

"The people who lived in the house were called the Bigelows. They gave me a code name, "Joe Wright," and helped me to leave Washington. A friend of theirs, Doctor H., took me to Philadelphia as his valet. Then another man took me to Buffalo, New York, as his son.

"The Underground Railroad sent a message to Reverend William King in Buxton, Canada West. Reverend King came to Buffalo to fetch me. He arranged a loud anti-slavery meeting right next to the Peace Bridge. As the border soldiers watched the noisy meeting, Reverend King and I slipped across the bridge to freedom."

Anne-Marie found the life she was looking for in Canada. She was adopted by a kind family, and lived on a farm near Buxton. After a while, she got married and had children of her own. She raised them in peace and freedom, thankful they would never know the cruel hardships of slavery.

TO CANADA WEST

In the 1840s, Red River was still the only European settlement between the Great Lakes and the Pacific. The Hudson's Bay Company had managed to keep settlers out of its vast western lands. The Company's huge fur-trading empire included most of today's Prairies, British Columbia, the Yukon and Northwest Territories.

In the 1850s, the Company's hold on its lands began to slip. *John Palliser* and Henry Hind each led surveying teams to find out more about the Western Prairies. Both teams found rich grasslands and reported that the Prairies were ripe for settlement. Settlers began to move westward to become pioneers on a new frontier.

In 1846, the western border between British North America and the United States was fixed at the 49th parallel. The Hudson's Bay Company had to move its west-coast headquarters north of this border. It chose *James Douglas* to build the new headquarters at Fort Victoria on Vancouver Island. Soon Vancouver Island was declared a British colony, with Douglas as its first governor.

In 1858, gold was found along the banks of the Fraser River. Word spread quickly, and gold-seekers poured into the area by the thousands. Douglas extended his control to the mainland and started a police force to keep order in the goldfields. In 1859, the mainland became the colony of British Columbia, with Douglas as its head.

European settlement brought many hardships to the Indians and Métis of the West. Settlers impinged on Native lands, spreading crime and disease. In many tribes, age-old ways of life began to disappear.

Most Native groups wanted to avoid war and bloodshed. Native spokesmen met with government leaders to discuss peacefully their claims to the land. The first treaties were signed and the first groups began to work for Native rights.

By the 1860s, the fur trade no longer had a hold on the West. Already, to the east in Canada, politicians were planning to include the West in their great scheme of union.

"The Victorian Pioneer Rifles." *James Douglas* invited refugee slaves to settle in his colony. He formed this all-Black regiment to help keep order in the goldfields. Douglas' own mother was probably a Black slave on a Caribbean plantation.

The Peace Chief

In the Cree language, "Maskepetoon" means "crooked arm." Perhaps, when he was young, Maskepetoon broke his arm while fighting. As a young warrior, he was known for his wild, violent temper.

As Chief Maskepetoon grew older, he began to see the value of peace. He grew to hate violence and looked for other ways to settle disputes among his people. Whenever he could, he made peace with enemy tribes and stopped his young braves from making war. He even met with the president of the United States to help make peace between the Cree and the Americans.

Though he loved peace, Maskepetoon did not always find it easy to control his anger. His own father was killed by a Blackfoot warrior. Later, Maskepetoon met the killer and had to fight back his rage. Then he welcomed the warrior into his lodge and gave him a chief's costume to show his forgiveness.

Chief Maskepetoon often acted as a guide for the Hudson's Bay Company. On one trip, he found an unexplored pass and followed it through the Rocky Mountains. In 1857, he guided *John Palliser*'s expedition through what is now southern Saskatchewan. Palliser called his guide *Nichiwa*, the Cree word for friend.

Maskepetoon loved peace so much he was even willing to die for it. In 1869, the Cree and Blackfoot were at war. Maskepetoon led a small party of Cree into a Blackfoot camp to discuss peace. He and his men were unarmed.

The Blackfeet warmly greeted Maskepetoon and invited him to sit down. Then a Blackfoot war chief gave a signal. The Blackfeet turned on the Cree and killed them. Maskepetoon died as a martyr to peace.

231

JOHN PALLISER   1817-1887

Opening the West

John Palliser was a big, burly Irishman who loved adventure. He was an educated man, who spoke five languages and sang in a rich tenor voice. In 1847, Palliser left England to hunt big game on the American plains.

2 Back in England, Palliser suggested a survey of the Canadian West. He won the support of the Royal Geographical Society and was placed in charge of a team of explorer-scientists.

1 Palliser fell in love with the North American Plains. He wrestled a bear with four-inch claws and was tossed on the horns of a bull buffalo. He left reluctantly, vowing to return someday.

3 In July 1857, Palliser's expedition began its journey across the plains. The explorers mapped the land and made careful notes on plants, animals, climate, and soil conditions. Palliser kept his men well supplied with buffalo meat.

4 Palliser was impressed with the Red River Valley and the lands along the North Saskatchewan River. He described these lands as a "fertile belt" where farms would someday prosper. He thought farms would do less well on the drier plains to the south.

6 In 1858, Palliser's team explored the Rockies to find a new route to the Pacific. One member, Dr. Hector, was kicked by his horse in a high mountain pass. His men were about to bury him when he blinked his eyes to show he was alive. Hector called the place Kicking Horse Pass.

5 Palliser and his men faced many hardships, but Palliser's spirits stayed high. When the group ran out of food, Palliser praised the quality of their tea. When they ran out of firewood, he cheerfully burned buffalo dung.

7 In less than three years, Palliser and his men explored over 750 000 square kilometres. Their favourable report caused Britain to change its policy and open up the West to settlement.

233

Mighty Man of the West

"Big Jimmy McKay" was a Métis, with a Scottish father and a Métis mother. Even as a young boy he was very strong. He went to work for the Hudson's Bay Company, guiding the Red River carts that moved supplies through the West. Many times he ploughed through waist-deep mud to drag horses and carts to safety.

McKay grew into a big man, and weighed over 140 kilograms. His feats of strength soon became legends. In one story, he rescued a newlywed couple who were stuck hopelessly in deep mud. He unhitched their horse, gave a mighty heave, and lifted up the cart, newlyweds and all!

McKay became an interpreter, trader, and guide with the Company. His fame grew, and soon many travellers wanted McKay as their guide across the West. *John Palliser* relied on McKay's guidance in the first year of his famous expedition. Even the head of the Hudson's Bay Company insisted on McKay as his guide.

One reason why McKay was such a good guide was his friendship with the western Indians. Many Indians were unwilling to let Europeans trespass on their lands. Often they only let Europeans through out of respect for McKay.

Even the Sioux, the traditional enemies of the Métis, saw McKay as their friend. When they were forced to flee the United States, many Sioux

pitched their teepees on McKay's land.

Because he knew many Indian languages, McKay played an important part in western treaty negotiations. He did all he could to see that his Indian friends got the best deal possible from the government.

In 1859, McKay married a woman who was almost his match for size. Margaret Rowand was a gracious, good-hearted woman from one of the richest families in the West. She and McKay built Deer Lodge, a beautiful mansion on the banks of the Assiniboine.

Deer Lodge soon became famous for its wonderful parties. Often the fiddlers played all night long, as young men in homespun trousers twirled their ladies round the dance floor.

In 1870, the new province of Manitoba was formed. McKay headed the Executive Council and became Speaker of the Assembly and Minister of Agriculture. Yet, no matter how powerful he became, McKay always dressed as a Red River Métis. He wore a blue *capot*, a red flannel shirt, homespun trousers, and brown moccasins.

McKay loved animals, and sometimes the grounds of Deer Lodge seemed like a zoo. When he saw how quickly the buffalo were disappearing, he brought some orphaned buffalo calves to Deer Lodge. This was the first buffalo herd to be raised off the plains.

After McKay died, his buffalo lived on. By the early 1900s, the prairie buffalo were almost extinct. The Canadian government used McKay's herd to keep the buffalo from dying out. Without the mighty McKay, there might not be any buffalo left alive today.

Father of British Columbia

As a schoolboy in Scotland, James Douglas loved stories about fur trading in the Canadian wilds. When he was 18, he joined the Hudson's Bay Company as a clerk.

In 1826, Douglas was sent to Fort St. James, west of the Rockies. He became assistant to William Connolly, chief factor of the region.

3 In 1843, Douglas supervised the building of Fort Victoria at the southern tip of Vancouver Island. In 1851, he became the first governor of the colony of Vancouver Island.

2 Douglas worked hard and rose quickly in the Company. In 1830, he went to Vancouver Island as assistant to John McLoughlin. When McLoughlin left, Douglas took over as chief factor.

1 Douglas soon fell in love with Amelia, the gentle daughter of Connolly and his Cree wife. When they married, Douglas was 25 and Amelia was 16.

4 Douglas built schools, churches, and a hospital in the little settlement at Victoria. At first, the colony grew very slowly. Then in 1858, gold was discovered on the mainland.

6 Douglas visited the goldfields himself. He issued mining licences, formed a police force, and appointed justices of the peace. He listened to complaints from Native people and made sure their rights were protected.

5 Victoria was soon invaded by thousands of fortune-seekers. Douglas knew that crime and violence often broke out in a gold rush. He acted quickly to keep order in Victoria and on the mainland.

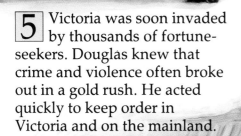

7 In 1858, Douglas became the first governor of British Columbia. For the next six years, he built roads and encouraged the growth of the new colony. He was knighted in 1864, and spent his last years in Victoria.

Salt Spring Settler

I see the hand of God, guiding me through all my troubles, guiding me to the higher life.

Sylvia Stark

Sylvia Stark was born a slave in the American state of Missouri. When she was 11, her father bought freedom for her family. He led them all on a six-month trek to the goldfields of California.

In California, Sylvia grew into a handsome young woman. She married Louis Stark and had two children of her own. At that time, Californian Blacks were often treated unfairly. Black children were barred from public schools, and Black people had few legal rights.

On Vancouver Island, *Governor James Douglas* heard about the hardships Black people were facing. He invited Black pioneers to come and settle in his colony. Sylvia packed up her family's few belongings and headed north to find a better life.

Sylvia and Louis decided to settle on Salt Spring Island, in the Strait of Georgia. This was a peaceful island of tall firs and arbutus trees, nestled amid calm green waters.

Over the years, Sylvia and her family managed to build a large, thriving farm. Sylvia loved to give away baskets of her fresh garden produce. She helped her neighbours any way she could. Often she worked as a volunteer nurse and midwife.

Sylvia Stark was in her nineties when she posed for the picture on this page. She refused to take off her apron to be photographed. After all, she said, she had worked hard all her life and was proud of it! She went on working hard, right up until her death at the age of 105.

GOLD!

Gold fever—it spread like wildfire, luring thousands with dreams of easy riches. In California, in Britain, even in China, goldseekers crowded into ships bound for the Fraser River goldfields. Saloon keepers and dancing girls followed close behind, hoping to cash in on the miners' luck.

The Fraser River goldrush got underway in 1858. Within weeks of the first gold strike, miners flooded into the area. Towns sprang up almost overnight in places no non-Native had ever been before.

James Douglas, the governor of Vancouver Island, acted quickly to bring law and order to the goldfields. With the help of *Judge Baillie Begbie*, he made the miners obey British laws. When British Columbia became a colony, Douglas became its first governor.

In late 1858, more gold was found further north in the Cariboo region. Miners raced to the area with their picks and shovels, and a second gold rush began. Some, like *Catherine Schubert*, came overland from the East. Others followed the new Cariboo Road up the treacherous Fraser Canyon.

Although Douglas kept order, these were still wild times. Miners went from poverty to riches and back again in a matter of weeks. Men fought wild brawls and squandered fortunes in saloons.

The Cariboo gold rush lasted until the mid-1860s. By then, most of the gold was gone. Miners who had not yet struck it rich began to realize they never would. Many of them put down their picks and shovels and took up ploughs. They became settlers in the new colony that the gold rush had helped to create.

"Prospecting for Alluvial Gold." *William Hind,* who painted this prospector, also tried panning for gold. His lack of success made him return to painting.

Overlander

Catherine was only 16 when she came to North America from Ireland. She married Augustus Schubert, a German pioneer full of schemes to get rich quickly. After a few years, the couple moved to the Red River settlement with their three children.

In May 1862, hundreds of gold seekers poured into Red River. These were the Overlanders, heading for the Cariboo goldfields of British Columbia. Augustus decided to join the Overlanders and seek his fortune. Catherine was expecting a baby, but she refused to stay behind.

"Muskeg near the Pembina River." These paintings by *William Hind* give a first-hand account of the Overlanders' ordeal. Catherine was the only woman among 138 men.

Over the next few months, Catherine Schubert travelled more than 3000 kilometres through rugged country. Here are some of the highlights of her epic journey.

June 2 —About 150 Overlanders leave Fort Garry, dragging 97 squeaking Red River carts. Catherine rides on horseback, with her two oldest children in baskets slung from her saddle. The group has set up a tight schedule. They will rise at 2:30 each morning and push off by 3:00.

June 25 —The Overlanders have lost their guide. As they head out across a vast trackless plain, mosquitoes and black flies swarm over them. Catherine's children cry, and she tries desperately to fan the insects away.

July 19—Rain has been pouring down for more than a week. The Overlanders' clothes are soaked, their blankets are damp, and their food is soggy. Today they must all wade neck-deep across a swollen torrent of water. When Catherine makes camp, she finds her tent is four inches deep in water.

August 6—The Overlanders reach the Pembina River, west of Fort Edmonton. Catherine ties her youngest child to her back, and urges her horse into the deep water. The horse's head jerks back and hits her in the face, knocking out one of her teeth.

August 19—The Overlanders have reached the Rocky Mountains. As they climb up steep cliffs, they are attacked by angry hornets. Two pack-horses miss their footing, and plunge over the side.

August 27—The Overlanders split into two groups. The largest will build rafts and brave the rapids of the Fraser River Canyon. Catherine sets out with the other group to follow the North Thompson River to Kamloops.

October 7—Catherine and her family are floating downstream on their raft. They are starving, living off roots, berries, and wild rosehips. They pass by an Indian village, and find the villagers dead from smallpox. In a nearby field, they find ripe potatoes to keep them alive.

October 13—Catherine reaches help just in time at a Shuswap village near Fort Kamloops. With help from the Shuswap women, she gives birth to a fine, healthy daughter. She calls her baby "Rose," after the rosehips that have helped keep her alive.

"Leather Pass" by *William Hind*. Soon after crossing the mountains, some of the Overlanders decided to brave the Fraser River. Catherine wanted to go with them, but her baby was almost due.

Rich Man, Poor Man

Billy Barker was a stocky little man with bandy legs and a bushy, black beard. Like most goldminers, he was a dreamer. He was 40 when he jumped ship at Victoria and headed for the Fraser goldfields. In 1862, he turned up at Williams Creek in the Cariboo.

Billy decided to dig for gold far downriver from the other miners. He found a place where he thought Williams Creek might have run in prehistoric times. The old-timers laughed at him as he dug his shaft deeper and deeper.

Soon Billy was working far below ground, digging with a pickaxe by candle-light. By the time his money ran out, his hole was 50 feet deep. Everyone told him he would never find any gold. Billy just shrugged and went on digging. He said he had been dreaming about the number 52.

At 52 feet, Billy Barker struck gold. He started taking out rich pans of gravel and gold, worth $5 each. Then, at 80 feet, he hit the motherlode. In two days he took out gold worth $1000.

Overnight, Billy became rich and famous. As word spread, miners streamed into the area. A raucous mining town sprang up, called Barkerville in Billy's honour. Billy began spending time in Barkerville saloons, dancing on the tables and singing this song:

> I'm English Bill,
> Never worked, never will,
> So get away, girls,
> Or I'll tousle your curls.

Billy married Elizabeth Collyer, a pretty widow who liked a good time. For the next three years, the couple squandered a fortune in dancing halls and gambling parlours. Then Billy's money ran out, and so did his wife. He spent the rest of his life in poverty and was buried in a pauper's grave.

A Man of His Word

It was October 1862, a bitter winter night in the Cariboo goldfields. In a lonely cabin, John Cameron watched as his wife, Sophia, lay dying. With great sorrow, he agreed to her last request. He would bury her close to her family, far away in Canada West.

At first Cameron was too busy digging for gold to keep his promise. Then, two months after Sophia's death, he struck paydirt. Soon people called him "Cariboo Cameron," one of the richest men in the Cariboo.

As Cameron grew rich, his conscience began to trouble him. He blamed himself for Sophia's death. He should never have brought her to the harsh Cariboo land.

In early 1863, Cameron set out at last to keep his promise. First, he loaded Sophia's coffin onto a sled. Then, he and some other men headed for Victoria, 1 000 kilometres away.

The first 600 kilometres were the worst. Deep snow covered the trails, and Cameron lost his way more than once. He had to sleep in the open, in temperatures that sometimes dropped to -50°C. He was caught in winter gales and fought his way through drifting snow.

At Victoria, Cameron had his wife's coffin filled with whiskey. This would preserve her body on its way through the tropics.

After some delay, Cameron loaded the coffin onto a steamship and set off for Panama. He crossed the Isthmus of Panama by train, then took another steamship to New York. By the time he

reached Cornwall, he had travelled over 15 000 kilometres!

Cariboo Cameron buried Sophia near her home in Cornwall, just as he had promised. Then he built himself a mansion and began to squander his fortune. When his money ran out, he went back to the Cariboo. He died there, poor and far from home.

The Riding Judge

Matthew Baillie Begbie was a tall, strong man with a restless streak in his nature. As a lawyer in London, he longed for a life of adventure. He was delighted when, in 1858, he became the first judge of the new colony of British Columbia.

When Begbie arrived at Vancouver Island, he found the gold rush in full swing.

2 Begbie wanted the law to reach every part of British Columbia. He travelled all over the huge colony by canoe, on horseback, and on foot. He held his trials in schoolhouses, barns, saloons, and in the open air.

3 In 1859, Begbie prepared the Gold Fields Act to regulate gold mining. He gave out copies and explained the law to gold miners and officials.

1 *Governor James Douglas* was happy to see Begbie. Thousands of gold-seekers were pouring into British Columbia and spreading havoc. Begbie looked just the man to bring order to the rough young colony.

4 Begbie made sure that Native Peoples in British Columbia were protected by British law. The Indians called him "Big Chief," and respected him for his fairness.

6 Many Chinese workers came to British Columbia to work on the Canadian Pacific Railway. Begbie defended Chinese rights, and rejected laws intended to drive them out.

5 Begbie fell in love with the rivers, mountains, and forests of British Columbia. An expert hunter and fisherman, he always tried to live off the land during long journeys.

7 Begbie was knighted in 1875. He built himself a fine home in Victoria, where he lived for the rest of his life. He never retired, but kept working as a judge until his death at age 75.

HOW THEY LIVED

Li Chan woke with a start. Someone was shaking him by the shoulder.

"Wake up, Li," whispered Choy. "It's time to go!"

Li had been dreaming of his father's rice fields in China. When he opened his eyes, he saw only the rough log walls of the way-house.

Li stood up and folded his blanket over the thin straw mattress. He followed Choy to the ladder of the sleeping loft. Then he climbed down to collect his supplies and pay the keeper of the way-house.

Li went out into Yale's main street and shivered in the cool dawn air. Li and Choy had come to Yale to pick up supplies for their group. They were miners, panning for gold on the banks of the Fraser River.

Li pushed his braid of black hair into the collar of his quilted jacket. Then he and Choy loaded the sacks of tea, rice, and flour into four wicker baskets. He would carry two of the baskets at the end of a pole slung across his shoulders.

As Li and Choy left Yale, the sun was just rising over the Fraser Canyon. Carefully, they followed a narrow, twisting path along the river's edge. Often the path was wet and slippery from river spray.

All that day, Li and Choy struggled toward their camp. By early evening, they were hungry and their backs hurt from carrying the baskets. Then, at last, they reached the place where their friends were panning for gold.

There were 12 other men in Li's group, all from the same part of China. Some of them hurried to greet Li and Choy. Others kept at their work, swirling gravel and water in pans, slowly emptying the pans until only gold was left at the bottom.

The miners' camp was on a narrow ledge above the river, barely big enough for their tents and campfire. Li squatted down by the fire and accepted a cup of tea. Then he told the others his big news.

"There's been a strike up north in the Cariboo!" he said. "Some of the miners are digging up thousands of dollars in gold!"

The younger men began to talk excitedly. Why settle for seven dollars a day, they asked, when they could all be millionaires? The older men were more cautious. They knew that for every millionaire, thousands came away with nothing. Some of them had also heard that Chinese miners were treated badly in the Cariboo.

The older men discussed the matter over a supper of rice and dried salmon. Then they told the group their decision. Some of the younger miners, including Li and Choy, would go on ahead to the Cariboo. If they made a big strike, the rest of the group would follow.

That night, as he curled up in his blanket, Li began to think of China. He would go to the Cariboo, and he would work hard to fill his baskets with gold. Then he would go home to China and build his father a fine new home.

For hundreds of years, men had sought the Northwest Passage through Canada's Arctic. At first, they had wanted a faster sea route to the rich spice lands of the Orient. Then, when that became less important, they searched for the Passage out of a love for adventure.

In 1845, *Sir John Franklin* led a British expedition to find the Passage. His ships were superbly equipped—in fact, they were over-equipped. When the ships became hopelessly locked in ice, some of the crew struck out over-land. They loaded tons of equipment onto huge sleds and began to drag them south. Along the way they died of hunger and exhaustion.

In Britain no one knew what had become of Franklin and his men. The British government spent millions of pounds searching for them. Explorers from many countries joined in the great Arctic manhunt.

Explorer *John Rae* found the first clues. Others, such as Charles Hall and his guides, *Ipilkvik* and *Tukkolerktuk*, filled in missing pieces. Gradually, the tragic story of Franklin and his men came to light.

Franklin's death taught European explorers an important lesson. Perhaps if he had not relied so much on his ships and supplies, he would have survived. Later explorers, like John Rae, would not make the same mistake. They would learn Arctic survival from the experts, the Indians and Inuit who lived there.

The search for Franklin sparked a whole new era of Arctic exploration. Explorers began once more to fill in the blank spaces on Arctic maps. Many took up a new challenge—the search for the North Pole.

This map was drawn in 1858 by Robert McClure, a British explorer. McClure was the first to travel the Northwest Passage from end to end.

Arctic Adventurer

Usually when we see the word "explorer," we think of a bold European adventurer. However, not all of Canada's explorers came from Europe. Over thousands of years, countless Indians and Inuit ventured bravely into unknown lands.

Kridlak was a great *angakok* (priest) who lived in northern Baffin Island. He heard a rumour from some whalers that another group of Inuit lived far to the north across Baffin Bay.

Kridlak began to dream of this faraway place and to visit it in visions. He gathered some of his people and set out to find the new land.

Kridlak led his group across Lancaster Sound and up the coast of Swan Island. They travelled slowly, hunting for their food with bows and harpoons. They faced blizzards and accidents on the dangerous ice, and survived long periods of hunger.

Year after year, Kridlak and his followers made their way slowly northward. They reached Ellesmere Island and spent six years travelling up its long treacherous coast. At last they came within 50 kilometres of Greenland. Kridlak followed his visions and led his people across the frozen sea.

Soon after Kridlak crossed into Greenland, he found the people he was searching for. He threw his weapons down in the snow and warmly greeted the Thule Inuit of Greenland. It was a great moment in the history of the Arctic.

Kridlak and his people stayed with the Thule in their village. They shared their hunting skills and mingled with the Thule through marriage. Today, the Thule Inuit and the Inuit of the northern Baffin Island think of themselves as one people.

The Tragic Explorer

whaling captain spotted Franklin's ships anchored to an ice floe in Baffin Bay. Then, Franklin and his men vanished into the lonely polar seas.

Over the next years, the British government spent millions of pounds searching for Franklin's ships. It was the biggest manhunt Canada's Arctic had ever seen. In 1854, explorer *John Rae* found the first clues, including some English silver bearing Franklin's crest.

In 1857, Franklin's wife, Lady Jane, sent out her own search party under Leopold McClintock. From his findings, and from tales told by the Inuit, the sad story was at last partly pieced together.

Sir John Franklin was delighted. The British were making one last search for the Northwest Passage through Canada's Arctic. Franklin was almost 60 and had already made his name as an Arctic explorer. Still, he would not rest until he was put in charge of the new expedition.

In May 1845, Franklin and his crew set sail in two sturdy ships. The *Erebus* and *Terror* were the strongest vessels that had ever been built for northern waters. They were equipped with a three-year supply of food, a library, and even a grand piano!

At first the voyage went well. The ships sailed easily across the North Atlantic, through Davis Strait, and into Baffin Bay. In July 1845, a

"Lady Jane Franklin." Lady Jane refused to abandon the search for her husband. When government expeditions failed to find him, she sent out a ship of her own.

"In Search of John Franklin" by William Bradford. The first Franklin-seekers repeated his mistake. Instead of travelling Inuit-style, they weighed themselves down with heavy ships and equipment.

Winter 1845–1846—Franklin's expedition spends a fairly comfortable first winter on Beechey Island in Lancaster Sound.

Summer 1846—Franklin sails south down Peel Sound and Franklin Strait. His ships try to pass King William's Island on the west, via Victoria Strait. Unknown to Franklin, Victoria Strait is blocked by ice year-round.

September 12, 1846—The *Erebus* and *Terror* become hopelessly trapped in the ice.

Winter 1846–1847—Over 700 large tins of meat have gone bad. Other provisions are dwindling. The men face a winter of food shortage, darkness, cold, and illness. They are still trapped in their ice-locked ships.

June 11, 1847—Sir John Franklin is dead. Perhaps he died of illness, or perhaps he met some accident on the treacherous ice. No one will ever know for sure.

April 25, 1848—At least 21 men have died. The others decide at last to abandon their trapped ships. Sick and starving, they load tons of equipment, including heavy boats, on huge sleds. They begin to walk south, hoping to reach fur traders on the mainland.

Over 100 men begin the walk. None of them reach their goal. Some die, exhausted, along the way. The rest leave a message on King William's Island, then struggle across the ice to a spot later called Starvation Cove. There, too weak to carry on, they perish.

An Arctic Survivor

John Rae joined the Hudson's Bay Company as a ship's doctor in 1833. Two years later, he became the Company's doctor at Moose Factory, on the shores of James Bay.

Rae soon came to love the harsh beauty of the Arctic wilderness. He spent much of his spare time exploring the countryside around the fort.

3 In 1847, Rae joined an expedition to search for *John Franklin*, the lost explorer. The other team members were badly trained and inexperienced. Rae found no trace of Franklin, but decided to try again.

1 Unlike other explorers, Rae learned Arctic survival skills from the Indians and Inuit. He made friends with a group of Swampy Cree and studied their language and way of life.

2 In 1846, Rae was asked to survey a stretch of Arctic coast. He gathered a team of skilled Inuit, Indians, Métis, and Scots. The expedition was a success, and Rae became a well-known Arctic explorer.

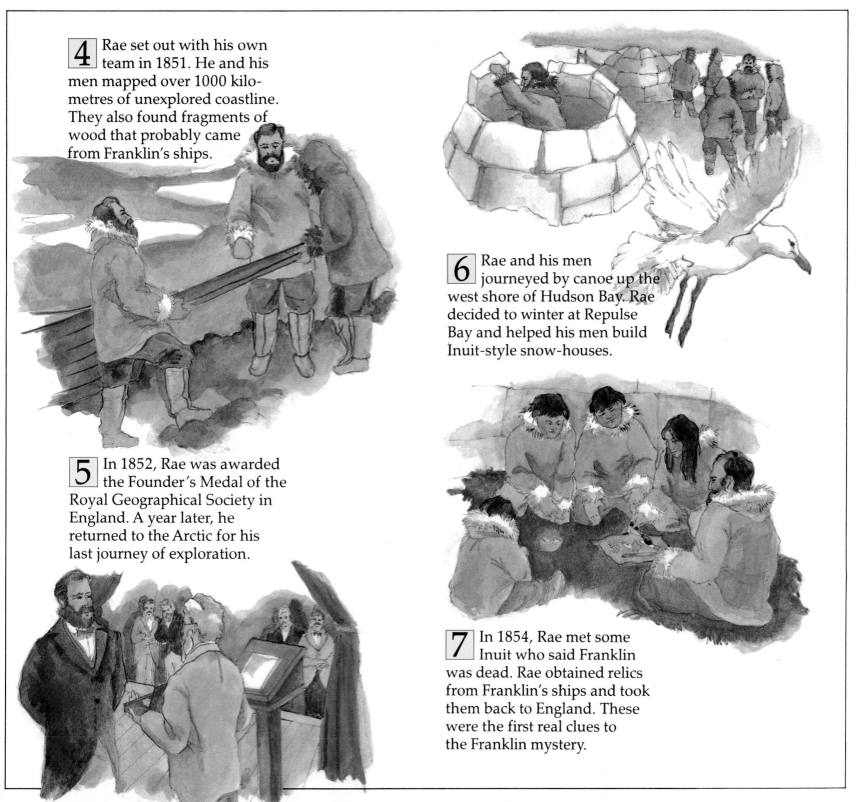

4 Rae set out with his own team in 1851. He and his men mapped over 1000 kilometres of unexplored coastline. They also found fragments of wood that probably came from Franklin's ships.

5 In 1852, Rae was awarded the Founder's Medal of the Royal Geographical Society in England. A year later, he returned to the Arctic for his last journey of exploration.

6 Rae and his men journeyed by canoe up the west shore of Hudson Bay. Rae decided to winter at Repulse Bay and helped his men build Inuit-style snow-houses.

7 In 1854, Rae met some Inuit who said Franklin was dead. Rae obtained relics from Franklin's ships and took them back to England. These were the first real clues to the Franklin mystery.

Explorers of the Far North

Ipilkvik and Tukkolerktuk were a young Inuit couple from Baffin Island. Both came from important Inuit families. The English whalers in the area called them "Joe and Hannah."

In 1858, Ipilkvik and Tukkolerktuk were invited to visit England. They spent almost two years there and learned to live like the English. They dined with Queen Victoria and met many famous and powerful people.

Back in the Arctic, the couple were happy to return to their own ways. They put their suits and dresses aside, and went back to a life of hunting and travelling.

In 1860, Ipilkvik and Tukkolerktuk became friends with Charles Hall, an American explorer. They invited Hall to live with them and learn their ways. They also visited Hall in the United States and helped him raise money for an Arctic expedition.

In 1864, the Inuit couple set out with Hall to search for *John Franklin*, the lost Arctic explorer. The group was put ashore at the wrong place. They spent a year struggling overland to Pelly Bay.

At Pelly Bay, the group met a band of hostile Inuit. Tukkolerktuk advised Hall to turn back, for she had heard that these people were dangerous. Then, at Repulse Bay, trouble broke out with some English whalers. Ipilkvik hid the whalers' guns and saved Hall's life.

In March 1869, the group set out again. Ipilkvik and Tukkolerktuk took along Pudnak, their adopted daughter. This time they found the place where Franklin had been lost. They took relics from Franklin's ships and heard how his men had starved in the snow.

In 1871, Ipilkvik and Tukkolerktuk set out with Hall to find the North Pole. When they reached the north coast of Greenland, Hall took sick and died. Their ship, *Polaris*, was stuck in pack-ice for the winter. Ipilkvik hunted for the crew and saved them from starvation.

In October 1872, the *Polaris* drifted into open water and struck a large ice floe. Everyone abandoned ship, and climbed onto the ice. For the next six months, they drifted south over 3000 kilometres.

Without Ipilkvik, the group would have starved. He built everyone snow-houses and made them lamps from pemmican cans. In the cold and dark, he hunted for seal and polar bears. He kept everyone alive until the spring, when they were rescued off the coast of Newfoundland.

After their ordeal on the ice, Ipilkvik and Tukkolerktuk settled down for a while in the United States. Then tragedy struck them. In 1875, Pudnak grew sick and died. Tukkolerktuk caught tuberculosis and died soon after. Sick with grief, Ipilkvik returned to the Arctic and never left there again.

WORDS AND PICTURES

The 1850s and 1860s were restless years for British North America. Life was changing faster than ever, and the young colonies were racing to keep up. From undersea telegraph cables in the East to bustling gold towns in the West, the colonies were alive with action.

Writers and artists thrived on the changes they saw around them. Some, like *William Hind*, wandered the country and sketched events as they happened. Others, like *Philippe Aubert de Gaspé*, tried to capture the past before it vanished completely.

For readers, changes in technology meant cheaper books and newspapers. By the 1860s, over 350 newspapers were published in British North America. One of the best was the *Provincial* magazine. Its editor, *Mary Jane Katzmann*, broke through barriers against women to become a leading force in the colonies.

Technology also influenced the other arts. Photographs became easier to take as new chemical processes were invented. Photographers everywhere left their studios to take pictures of the world around them. In the Prairies, *Humphrey Lloyd Hime* dragged along his equipment by dogsled and Red River cart. His pictures were the first to be taken in the Canadian West.

"Behind Bonsecours Market, Montreal." William Raphael painted this lively scene of immigrants milling in Montreal's marketplace. Raphael was an immigrant himself from eastern Europe. He was Canada's first well-known Jewish artist.

MARY JANE KATZMANN   1828–1890

Woman of Letters

Mary Jane Katzmann grew up in Nova Scotia in an age when few women had successful careers. Mary Jane decided to be different. She taught herself history, languages, and literature. She wrote poems for the newspapers and was encouraged by *Joseph Howe*.

2 In the mid-1860s, Mary Jane opened the Provincial Bookstore in Halifax. The store was a success and became one of the province's leading literary centres.

1 When she was 24, Mary Jane became editor of the *Provincial*, a new magazine. She printed stories, poems, and good local articles on travel, science, and history. The *Provincial* soon became the finest journal in Nova Scotia.

3 When she was 40, Mary Jane married and returned to her own writing. Her finest work was her award-winning history of the Dartmouth area of Halifax County. Her colourful account of life in early Nova Scotia can still be read today.

Painter of Habitant Life

Cornelius Krieghoff was a hearty, fun-loving man, who loved to see people enjoy themselves. As a boy in Germany, he learned to paint and play the violin. Later he studied art in the great cities of Europe, playing music in taverns to pay his way.

In 1837, Krieghoff sailed for New York City. There he fell in love with Louise Gauthier, a pretty French Canadian. Louise told Krieghoff of the beauty of her country, with its clear lakes and wooded hillsides. Krieghoff married Louise and took her north to settle near her home in Canada.

The first few years were hard ones for the newlyweds. First in Toronto, then in Montreal, Krieghoff struggled to make a living. He went from door to door, trying to sell his paintings for $5 or $10. He painted store signs and took work as a housepainter to support his family.

Krieghoff's luck began to change in 1854, when he moved to Quebec City. Krieghoff was enchanted with the countryside around Quebec. He delighted in the rich colours of the autumn woods. In winter, he loved the dazzling white of the snow-covered fields and hills.

During the next 11 years, Krieghoff painted hundreds of scenes of country life. He was very popular with the habitants he met. Often he played the fiddle at their parties and dances.

Krieghoff gloried in the colour and gaiety of habitant life. He painted bustling farmwives and frolicking children, tumbledown farmhouses and horse-drawn sleighs. He visited many country

"Self-Portrait." Krieghoff painted this portrait of himself at 43 just before he became successful.

inns and sketched the habitants as they danced and sang.

At first the well-to-do people of Quebec City disliked Krieghoff's paintings. They wanted to see pictures of their own grand homes and fine parties. They thought Krieghoff was wasting his time painting rough-and-ready scenes of farm life.

As time passed, however, Krieghoff's paintings became more "fashionable." English officers began to buy them to send back to England as souvenirs. Even *Lord Elgin*, governor of Canada, asked Krieghoff to paint his portrait.

In 1862, Krieghoff left his home in Quebec City. He probably went to live with his daughter in Chicago. Kreighoff soon began to miss the beauty and gaiety of the countryside near Quebec. In the next years, he painted fewer and fewer pictures. He died at the age of 57, far from the land he loved.

"The Blacksmith's Shop." Krieghoff's paintings are full of colourful details of daily habitant life. Notice the dog barking at the horse and the child peeking through the curtains.

Poet and Patriote

As our flag passes by, its radiant light
Kindles our souls with the blazing sight
Of our forefathers, and the glories of
    another time.
Their great days of battle, their immortal
    deeds,
Their superhuman struggle, their
    sorrows and defeats,
All these pass before us like a dream.

> from "The Flag of Carillon,"
> by Octave Crémazie

Octave Crémazie was just fifteen years old when the 1837 Patriote Rebellion broke out in Lower Canada. The young boy longed to join his people's struggle for freedom from British rule. He was very sad when the Patriotes were defeated.

When Crémazie was 17, he finished school and opened a bookstore with his brother. The Crémazie bookstore soon became the most important cultural centre in Quebec City. Important writers, such as *François-Xavier Garneau*, gathered there to learn from one another.

Like Garneau, Crémazie was very proud of his heritage. He was afraid that French Canadians would abandon their traditions under British rule. He hated to think of his countrymen as a conquered people.

Crémazie began to write poems to celebrate French Canada's history. He wrote of the glories of French Canada's past, praising its heroes and its warriors. All over Canada East, people began to read Crémazie's poems. Men and women discussed them eagerly, and children learned them by heart. French Canadians began to take new pride in their past.

Tragically, Crémazie had to leave the land he loved. When he was just 40, he ran deeply into debt and fled to France. For the rest of his life, he lived in exile, longing to return home.

Crémazie never wrote another poem after he left Quebec. "The finest poems," he said, "are those we dream of but do not write."

A Canadian of Old

Philippe Aubert de Gaspé grew up in wealth and luxury. He became a successful young lawyer and the sheriff of Quebec City. Then, when he was 38, he suddenly went bankrupt.

To avoid prison, Philippe took his family to his mother's country estate. He spent the next 14 years in exile there, reading about his country's past. He got to know the local habitants and learned their folksongs and legends.

2 After he was released, Philippe joined Quebec City's literary world. He started writing a historical novel, *Canadians of Old*. He filled his book with the customs and folklore of old New France.

1 In 1838, Philippe was arrested for debt. He spent the next three years in a cold, dark prison cell. To pass the time, he recalled the songs and stories he had heard.

3 Philippe was 76 when he finished *Canadians of Old*. He then wrote his *Memoires* about his colourful life in the early 1800s. Both books were wildly popular and helped keep French Canada's culture alive.

The Wandering Artist

"Self-portrait."

William Hind was a moody, restless man, always looking for new experiences. He was part painter and part explorer. He loved to travel to new places and paint scenes that no one had painted before.

Hind was 19 when he came to Canada to stay with his brother, Henry. He spent a few years teaching art in Toronto. He tried without much luck to sell his paintings there.

In 1861, Henry left to explore and survey the interior of Labrador. Hind joined his brother, and made sketches of the trip to illustrate Henry's report. He enjoyed the rugged travel through unexplored countryside, and he painted many scenes of Indian life.

Hind's trip to Labrador whetted his appetite for adventure. He left Toronto and headed west for the Cariboo goldfields of British Columbia. He joined the Overlanders, a group of goldseekers that included *Catherine Schubert* and her three children.

The Overlanders' journey was long and hard. The goldseekers waded through muskeg swamps and slept in rain-soaked tents. They faced charging buffalo and dense plagues of mosquitoes. They hacked their way through thick bush and inched their way up treacherous mountain paths. They even built rafts and shot the murderous rapids of the Fraser Canyon.

Hind did not make the journey any easier for himself. He became moody and quarrelsome, and argued with his tentmates. After one quarrel, he was forced to travel on his own for several days.

"Duck Hunting." Hind travelled throughout Canada and painted many of its landscapes. He painted forests, sea coasts, mountains, and the lush green oceans of prairie grassland.

"Bar in Mining Camp." Hind's paintings are doorways in time, giving us vivid glimpses of the past. In this Caribou saloon, we can almost smell the stale smoke as disappointed miners drown their sorrows.

Through it all, Hind sketched and painted. In his pictures, he caught the Overlanders stumbling through woods and fording through icy rivers. He showed them making pemmican and relaxing with a game of cards. He painted them as they struck camp and as they dragged their carts through swampy river beds.

In all, Hind made over 160 finely detailed sketches and paintings of the journey. They offer a brilliant record of one of the greatest adventures in Canada's history.

Hind never struck gold in the Cariboo, but he did paint many wonderful pictures of mining life. He painted grizzled old miners and raw, unshaven boys. He showed them panning at the goldfields, drinking in saloons, and swapping songs and stories around the campfire.

After a few years, Hind left the West. He spent the rest of his life in the Maritimes, working for railways and sketching the countryside. He painted several pictures of the divers who laid the first undersea telegraph cables.

Few people appreciated Hind's pictures in his lifetime. After his death, most of them were lost or forgotten. Some ended up as dartboards and were shot full of holes. Then, almost 100 years after his death, Hind's paintings were found and hailed as masterpieces.

First Photographer in the West

In the 1850s, photographers did much more than point a camera and press a button. They needed all kinds of clumsy, heavy equipment to take their pictures. Most photographers stayed in their studios, where they had everything they needed. Some, like Humphrey Lloyd Hime, were more adventurous and dragged their equipment with them.

Hime was born in Ireland, and came to Toronto as a photographer and engineer. In 1858, Henry Hind invited him to join his expedition to explore and survey the West. Hind's surveyors wanted to find out if the lands west of Red River

should be settled. Hime went along to take photos of the journey to illustrate Hind's report.

Hime needed a great deal of equipment to take his pictures. His box camera was huge and awkward to carry. He used many lenses, all needing protection from the cold and damp. He needed a sturdy tripod to keep the camera steady while it exposed each shot. Instead of film, he carried caseloads of heavy glass plates.

Hime also needed many different chemicals to develop his pictures. He needed plate holders,

"Encampment of the Henry Hind Expedition" by H. L. Hime. This was probably the first photograph to be taken west of Lake Superior. It was shot on the banks of the Red River.

"Laetitia Bird, a Swampy Cree." Hime's portraits of Indians and Métis are considered masterpieces of early photography.

scales, rinsing pails, and other paraphernalia. He used black sheets and a dark tent for an on-the-spot darkroom.

Hime somehow managed to carry his equipment and supplies by canoe and Red River cart. Sometimes he portaged for miles around rapids, carrying his equipment on his back. Other times he dragged it on carts across muskeg and through swampy rivers.

Most of Hime's pictures were lost on the trip. Some fell into the water during a dangerous river crossing. Others were damaged by torrential rains and plagues of locusts. Those that survived were the first photographs ever taken of Canada's West.

Despite all his hardships, Hime's photos turned out brilliantly. Many of them show the simple dignity of life on the Western frontier. His fine portraits of Native people have been called masterpieces of early photography.

Soon after Hime returned from the West, he quit work as a photographer. He became a stockbroker, and rose to become president of the Toronto Stock Exchange. Perhaps, after his journey, photography seemed too hard a life. He never worked as a photographer again.

ONE CANADA

As co-premiers of the Province of Canada, *John A. Macdonald* and *Georges Cartier* had very hard jobs. Somehow they had to satisfy both the French-speaking voters of Canada East and the English-speaking voters of Canada West. Yet the two groups could hardly ever agree!

Macdonald and Cartier thought their problem could be solved by the union of all the British North American colonies. Within the union, each province could control its own interests, such as schools and hospitals. Then a central government could deal with wider problems such as trade and defence. People of very different backgrounds and beliefs began to work for Confederation.

In 1864, Macdonald, Cartier, and others presented their plan to Maritime delegates at the Charlottetown Conference. They found strong support from *Charles·Tupper* of Nova Scotia and *Samuel Tilley* of New Brunswick. A month later, leaders met in Quebec City and approved "72 Resolutions" that formed the basis for union.

In the Atlantic colonies, many people disliked the idea of Confederation. Newfoundland and Prince Edward Island refused outright to join. In Nova Scotia and New Brunswick, Tupper and Tilley seemed to be fighting a losing battle. Then they had a stroke of luck.

A group of Irish Fenians tried to invade the colonies and hand them over to the United States. Many people in Nova Scotia and New Brunswick were outraged. In a burst of angry patriotism, the colonies agreed to join Confederation.

On July 1, 1867, the Dominion of Canada was officially born. As its motto it took the words "a mari usque ad mare," or " from sea to sea."

"The Fathers of Confederation at the Quebec Conference of 1864." This painting shows a meeting which never actually took place. The three men on the right only attended the London Conference of 1866.

SIR SAMUEL LEONARD TILLEY   1818–1896

New Brunswick's Leader in Confederation

Samuel Tilley left school at 13 to become a druggist. He entered politics in 1850 and became premier of New Brunswick in 1861. In 1864, Tilley attended the Charlottetown Conference. He heard *John A. Macdonald* call for a union of all British North American colonies. Tilley thought union would be good for New Brunswick, so he gave Macdonald strong support.

1 Tilley took his arguments directly to the people. He travelled all over New Brunswick, speaking passionately for union. Despite his speeches, however, most New Brunswickers still opposed Confederation.

2 In 1865, Tilley's support for union cost him an election. Soon after, Irish Fenians threatened to invade the Maritimes and stop Confederation. New Brunswickers were outraged and gave Tilley all the support he needed.

3 In 1866, Tilley helped write the British North America Act. The next year, he led New Brunswick into Confederation. Tilley suggested the title, "Dominion of Canada," and the motto "from sea to sea."

Canada's First Prime Minister

"I hear you have a smart man up there—John A. Macdonald," said the American senator's wife. She was chatting with a tall gangling fellow from Canada. "They say Macdonald's a real scalawag though," she went on. "Why do the Canadians keep such a man in power?"

"Well," came the reply, "They just can't seem to get on without him!"

At that moment, the American senator came over and introduced his wife to her tall companion. "My dear," he began, "May I present Sir John A. Macdonald?"

Macdonald was a bit of a scalawag, but he was also a great leader. He had a strong, clear mind, and he inspired love and loyalty in others. He had great charm and a gift for making people feel important. As a speaker, he was famous for his funny stories and witty replies to hecklers.

Macdonald was born in Scotland and grew up in Kingston, Canada West. When he was 15, he left school to work in a law office. He entered politics in 1843 and rose quickly in the Conservative Party.

Around this time, Macdonald married his gentle half-cousin, Isabella Clark. He adored his new wife, and for a while they were happy together. Then Isabella began to grow ill. She gave birth to two sons, but one of them died in infancy.

Isabella became an invalid, confined to her bed for long cruel years of suffering. Macdonald began to drink heavily and threw himself into his work.

In 1857, Isabella died. That same year, Macdonald became premier of the Province of Canada. His co-leader was *Georges Cartier*, head of French Canada's Conservatives.

Macdonald's first wife, Isabella (A) died young after a long illness. Their son, Hugh John (B), later became Manitoba's premier. Macdonald married his second wife, Susan Agnes (C), a few months before Confederation. Their daughter, Mary, was an invalid all her life.

"The Queen's Tribute." Several months before Confederation, Queen Victoria met with Macdonald and four other Canadians in London.

Along with others, Macdonald began to push for the union of British North America. He built support in the Province of Canada, then headed for the Maritimes to find support there. At the Charlottetown Conference of 1864, he regaled the Maritimers with speeches by day and champagne parties by night.

During the next years, Macdonald and the others perfected their plans for union. Macdonald wrote most of the 72 Resolutions that formed the basis of Confederation. First at Quebec, then in Britain, he led the colonies into nationhood.

On July 1, 1867, Nova Scotia, New Brunswick, and the Province of Canada united to form the Dominion of Canada. John A. Macdonald was knighted and became Canada's first prime minister.

Macdonald's life was still far from over. Through the next decades, his life was filled by many more triumphs and sorrows. He began a new, happy marriage with Susan Agnes Bernard. He saw his daughter born with a cruel disease and confined to a wheelchair for life. He lost an election and returned in triumph to build the Canadian Pacific Railway.

Macdonald never let himself get beaten by his troubles. He even gave a piece of advice to some friends: "Be philosophical, and if Fortune empties a chamberpot on your head, just smile and say, 'We are having a summer shower!'"

Nova Scotia's Fighting Doctor

When he was a boy, Charles Tupper loved a good fight. He was afraid of no one, and he threw himself headlong into his battles. He grew up in Amherst, Nova Scotia, with more than his share of black eyes and bruised knees. Even as a young Amherst doctor, he got into a few scraps.

Perhaps it was Tupper's love of fighting that drew him into politics. In those days, elections often broke into rough-and-tumble fights. Some voters armed themselves with clubs in case they were attacked at the polls.

In 1855, Tupper ran for election in Cumberland County against the legendary *Joseph Howe*. The people of Cumberland loved Howe, but they loved their country doctor more. After all, it was Tupper who came out on freezing nights to care for their sick families.

Tupper won the election, and soon began to rise in Nova Scotia's government. He travelled the country, spreading his dream of union for the colonies of British North America. In 1864, he became leader of Nova Scotia's Conservative party. At the same time, he became premier of Nova Scotia.

As soon as he became premier, Tupper helped to organize the Charlottetown Conference. At the conference, he began his long friendship with *John A. Macdonald*. Tupper shared Macdonald's vision of a united nation, stretching from sea to sea. At the Quebec Conference, he helped to hammer that vision into a reality.

In 1866, Irish Fenians tried to invade the colonies of British North America and stop Confederation. Nova Scotians were outraged. Many began to feel they needed the united strength that Confederation would provide.

Tupper took full advantage of this change, and pushed for a vote on Confederation. In April 1866, Nova Scotia's parliament voted 31 to 19 in favour of union. The next year, on July 1, 1867, Nova Scotia became a province in the new nation of Canada.

Tupper still had to win over many Nova Scotians who opposed Confederation. He agreed not to enter Macdonald's cabinet until more Nova Scotians were behind him. He invited Joseph Howe to work alongside him to protect Nova Scotia's interests. At last, Howe agreed to join Macdonald's cabinet. Only then did Tupper accept a cabinet post for himself.

Tupper served for many years in Canadian politics. He supervised the building of the Canadian Pacific Railway, and represented Canada in England. In 1896, he became leader of the Conservative Party. That same year, he became Canada's prime minister.

Now Tupper really had a fight on his hands. Joseph Howe believed that union would be disastrous for Nova Scotia. He called Confederation the "Botheration Scheme" and bitterly attacked it in the newspapers. He and his supporters turned most Nova Scotians against Confederation.

Tupper chose his moment, then threw himself into the battle. He stormed through the province, praising the idea of union. He confronted angry, heckling audiences, and made fiery speeches to win their support.

SIR GEORGES-ETIENNE CARTIER   1814–1873

Patriote and Nation Builder

As a young lawyer, Georges Cartier resented the unfair treatment of French Canada by the British. He joined the Patriotes, a group of French Canadians led by *Louis-Joseph Papineau*. In 1837, the Patriotes took up arms against their British rulers. Cartier left his law practice and joined in the rebellion.

3 In 1857, the *Macdonald-Cartier* government was formed. As leader for Canada East, Cartier fought for French Canadian rights. He thought these rights would be safer within a union of all British North America.

1 Cartier fought bravely at the Battle of Saint-Denis. When the uprising failed, he fled into exile in the United States. In 1858, he returned to his law practice in Montreal.

2 In 1848, Cartier was elected to the Assembly for Canada East. In the next years, he introduced many reforms in education and justice.

4 For the sake of unity, Cartier made peace with many of his political enemies in English Canada. Conservatives and Reformers began to work together for Confederation.

5 Cartier was French Canada's chief spokesman at the Charlottetown and Quebec Conferences. He made sure that a strong provincial government would represent its needs.

6 In London, Cartier was a major force behind the British North America Act. Macdonald said later that without Cartier, there would have been no Confederation.

7 Like most people in Ottawa, Cartier celebrated when Confederation was declared in 1867. He was knighted the next year, and he continued to serve Canada until his early death at 59.

Founder of The Globe

George Brown was a large, vigorous man, with a booming voice and strong opinions. When he was only 25, he started the *Globe* to spread his political ideas. The *Globe* soon became the most powerful newspaper in British North America. Today, we know it as the *Globe and Mail*.

George Brown was a Reformer who wanted more power for Canada West. Under his leadership, the Reform Party grew very strong and powerful. Brown was a tough fighter who did not like compromise. He made many enemies in the Conservative Party, including *John A. Macdonald*, *Georges Cartier*, and *D'Arcy McGee*.

In the 1860s, Brown's opinions began to mellow. He fell in love with Anne Nelson, and asked her to be his wife. With Anne beside him, he began to lose interest in his political quarrels.

In 1864, Brown offered to work with John A. Macdonald for Confederation. The two men made peace with what has been called "the most important handshake in Canadian history."

Brown worked hard at Charlottetown and Quebec to develop plans for Confederation. He designed the federal-provincial system that became the basis for Canada's government. However, Brown's heart was no longer in politics. In 1866, he decided to resign. With relief, he wrote to Anne, "I am a free man once again."

Brown continued to shape ideas through his work as editor of the *Globe*. Then, when he was

61, tragedy struck. A *Globe* worker, who had been fired for drunkenness, pushed into Brown's office with a gun. Like his old enemy, D'Arcy McGee, Brown died of an assassin's bullet.

"George Brown Addresses a Crowd." Brown was much loved in Upper Canada. When he brought his bride back from England, his supporters paraded joyfully through Toronto streets.

THOMAS D'ARCY McGEE   1825–1868

Silver-Tongued Statesman

D'Arcy McGee grew up in Ireland, a poet and a rebel. As a young man, he spoke out passionately against British rule in Ireland. In 1848, he was arrested for taking part in an Irish rebellion. When the rebellion failed, he fled to the United States disguised as a priest.

"Funeral Procession of the late Thomas D'Arcy McGee." Patrick Whalen was convicted of killing McGee but many believe he was innocent. The execution was Canada's last public hanging.

In 1857, a group of Irish Canadians invited McGee to move to Montreal. He accepted and started his own newspaper, the *New Era*. In 1858, he became a member of parliament for Montreal. At first he opposed the Conservative Party and its leader, *John A. Macdonald*.

McGee had a great gift for words, and he soon became famous as a speaker. His radical views mellowed, and he began to work for the union of British North America. In 1863, he joined the Conservatives in their drive toward Confederation. He travelled through the colonies, firing his audiences with passionate speeches.

McGee spoke brilliantly at the Charlottetown and Quebec Conferences of 1864. He also helped draw up the 72 Resolutions that formed the basis of Canada. He worked hard to make sure the new country would honour the rights of minorities.

In 1864, Irish Fenian rebels tried to invade British North America. They hoped to hurt Britain by turning her colonies over to the United States. McGee spoke out against the attack and made many enemies in the Irish community.

In 1867, the Dominion of Canada was born. However, D'Arcy McGee did not live long enough to see the new country mature. On April 7, 1868, at 2:30 in the morning, he was shot down in the street outside his rooming house. The assassination was thought to be a Fenian plot. A young Irishman named Patrick Whalen was publicly hanged for the murder.

Index